Awakening the Energy Body

"This is a brilliant articulation of our limitless possibilities and how to realize them. *Awakening the Energy Body* is based on the entire history of inquiry into energetics, up to and including the findings of modern science. The book will vastly expand your comprehension of your own energy system and what it means to you and all your relationships. The fascinating journey of discovery described here is the most important story you can know about; it will impact every moment of your life. Prepare to discover the vast if not infinite resources that are available to all of us."

JAMES L. OSCHMAN, PH.D., AUTHOR OF
ENERGY MEDICINE: THE SCIENTIFIC BASIS

"Kenneth Smith's synthesis of Toltec philosophy and energetic anatomy is breathtaking in its scope. Drawing on both ancient teachings and the latest technological scientific advances, *Awakening the Energy Body* challenges contemporary assumptions about the nature of reality, the metaphysical structure of the human body, and the limits of knowledge. His insights break new ground in the fields of philosophy, health, psychology, mind/brain studies, and spirituality. This is a book that deserves to be read widely and thought about deeply."

PAUL RADEMACHER, M.DIV.,
EXECUTIVE DIRECTOR OF THE MONROE INSTITUTE

"What a great mind-stretcher. Or, perhaps I should better say a great energy-stretcher."

CHARLES T. TART, PH.D., PROFESSOR EMERITUS OF PSYCHOLOGY,
UNIVERSITY OF CALIFORNIA, DAVIS

"Kenneth Smith has methodically and thoughtfully written what may lead us toward a revolution of thought and consciousness. Whether or not you are a scientist, practitioner, or layperson this book has something for you. I wish I had it years ago."

ERIK FISHER, PH.D., AUTHOR OF
THE ART OF EMPOWERED PARENTING

"Kenneth Smith's *Awakening the Energy Body* illuminates the essential nature of being human, illustrates the basic mechanisms that we use to form separate realities, and offers us deeper understanding for establishing a healthier relationship in the world. This amazing book demonstrates the universality of the energy body by relating its dynamics to psychology, physics, sociology, and religion; and it helps to further establish the fields of bioenergetics, Energy Psychology, and Transpersonal Psychology. I can imagine the Toltec shaman don Juan announcing that *Awakening the Energy Body* offers us more than an ordinary path through the woods, since this is a path with true heart."

FRED GALLO, PH.D., AUTHOR OF *ENERGY TAPPING*

"Kenneth Smith eloquently reveals what we all need to know regarding the energy body—its nature, functions, and purpose. By embracing this perennial wisdom we are offered the rarest of opportunities: to once again experience the practical philosophy of the sage, the seer, and the shaman."

SIMON BUXTON, AUTHOR OF *THE SHAMANIC WAY OF THE BEE*

"This book presents a natural and spontaneous way to explore one's awakening potential. If you've ever wanted to pick up an easy to understand guide for following in the footsteps of a Toltec Master, this is it."

JOSEPH W. MCMONEAGLE, AUTHOR OF
REMOTE VIEWING SECRETS

"In the tradition of Carlos Castañeda, Kenneth Smith applies the energy body concept to a broad expanse of the academic landscape. The reader who participates in the spiritual exercise of this book will see the world differently."

JAMES F. DRANE, PH.D., RUSSELL B. ROTH PROFESSOR OF BIOETHICS,
EDINBORO UNIVERSITY OF PENNSYLVANIA

"If you want to change your life, simply change your mind. This simple truth is perhaps the greatest tool for personal change that remains unknown by most of the contemporary world. My hope is that *Awakening the Energy Body* might contribute to the understanding that we truly have a major role in cocreating our lives and our world, and it is a role that we can no longer neglect to take seriously."

KEVIN J. TODESCHI, AUTHOR OF
EDGAR CAYCE ON VIBRATIONS

Awakening
the
Energy Body

FROM SHAMANISM TO BIOENERGETICS

Kenneth Smith

Bear & Company
Rochester, Vermont

Bear & Company
One Park Street
Rochester, Vermont 05767
www.BearandCompanyBooks.com

Bear & Company is a division of Inner Traditions International

Library of Congress Cataloging-in-Publication Data
Smith, Kenneth.
  Awakening the energy body : from shamanism to bioenergetics / Kenneth Smith.
    p. cm.
  Includes bibliographical references and index.
  ISBN 978-1-59143-084-1 (pbk.)
  1. Awareness. 2. Consciousness. 3. Shamanism. 4. Bioenergetics. 5. Energy psychology. I. Title.

  BF311.E235 2008
  131—dc22

                                                          2008008235

Printed and bound in the United States by Lake Book Manufacturing

10 9 8 7 6 5 4 3 2 1

Text design and layout by Jon Desautels
This book was typeset in Garamond Premier Pro

To send correspondence to the author of this book, mail a first-class letter to the author c/o Inner Traditions • Bear & Company, One Park Street, Rochester, VT 05767, and we will forward the communication.

You may also contact the author through his website, www.biocognition.net.

To Emma,
my beloved daughter,
and to her generation—
With thine maps
may thee securely saile.

Contents

Preface

"Reality" is a human-made construct. It is a description of the world, born of imagination and defined by learning. Whether a view of reality is based on science, philosophy, religion, or something else, it is a single canvas in a museum or one book in a magnificent library.

Each view of reality changes over time as individuals, groups, and the species evolve. What remains consistent is that the reality we experience is based on our current perceptions of what we think reality is. Since birth, we have each performed intricate maneuvers of learning, building, and consolidating a worldview. This is quite an accomplishment, even though we have created only a partial reflection of the vastness that lies before us all.

The truth is that creation far exceeds our capacity to grasp it. Human-made reality is therefore a practical framework that enables us to survive and continue learning. Learning and survival go hand in hand. But to this end the current worldview is problematic. It is possible that humans are at a crossroads, requiring a change in our view of the world to survive. Global warming, which has occurred as a direct result of human-made reality, is not only threatening social structures of all kinds but also the very existence of many forms of life on this planet. In a similar way, centuries ago a European "flat earth" view prevented exploration of other continents and oceans. Learning was stultified as a result. Lack of awareness caused the beneficial and detrimental effects of both viewpoints, modern and historical.

Answers to our contemporary challenges are emerging, however. People are growing more aware of the causes and impacts of global warming. Organizations are taking up arms on behalf of endangered species. And ethical debates abound. Hopefully, my contribution is that of providing information about a unique philosophy of learning, which offers the possibility of heightened awareness and an expanded worldview.

Writing under the name Ken Eagle Feather, I have published five books about Toltec philosophy and theory, a branch of shamanism in which the energy body is a principal component.[1] Over some thirty years, I have found that ancient Toltec teachings reveal the inherent processes of perception, including how we form reality. These teachings do not exist in a vacuum. In modern terms, they are rightfully an extension of established fields in psychology, philosophy, and bioenergetics. They do, however, serve to expand the boundaries of accepted knowledge.

Others have also written about Toltec views and practices, elevating a once-hidden philosophy to a more recognizable position among an array of metaphysical literature. Since Carlos Castaneda's first book, *The Teachings of Don Juan*, was published in the late 1960s, Toltec literature has gained ever-widening, international recognition.[2] While Castaneda and his books gained a significant degree of notoriety, his work in providing an emic account (from the point of view of a participant rather than an outside, "objective" observer) of Toltec teachings earned him a doctorate in anthropology from UCLA.[3] Toltec practitioners such as Victor Sanchez, Florinda Donner, Taisha Abelar, Miguel Ruiz, Susan Gregg, and others have contributed to an ever-growing body of work.

Awakening the Energy Body is not a "Toltec" book as such; that is, there are no practices related solely to that body of knowledge. Rather, it presents those aspects of the energy body that apply to everyone, not just to those with esoteric inclinations. It takes the essence of what

Toltec shamans discovered regarding the basic structure of the human energy body—especially as it relates to individual and group learning and development—and then looks at it through a lens of contemporary understanding. Particular attention is given to the rapidly expanding discipline of bioenergetics, which studies the flow and exchange of energy, a field that nicely meshes with advances in the scientific understanding of cognition and consciousness. The combination of shamanism and bioenergetics in this book provides a significant stepping-stone to increased awareness of the physiological and psychological aspects of human behavior.

A few of the topics covered are projection, stages of awakening, learning, imagination, fundamentalism, altered states of consciousness, and the ontological state of *being*. I have found that not being aware of our personal energy body is like trying to walk down the street without the use of our legs. Developing this awareness results in a profound shift in the way the world is viewed and subsequent changes in behavior. This enhanced relationship with our world permits additional learning, including new ways to learn.

Learning hinges on how well you use the tools available to you as well as having the tools at your disposal in the first place. You may have large amounts of perspective and not have any experience that matches that context. Likewise, you might have plenty of experience that goes to waste because you don't have the means to apply and integrate the experience. This text will provide you with perspectives such as the Stages of Awakening or Ontological Development (in chapter 4), which will guide you in knowing how and where to aim your resources and experiences, and offer a way to gauge how you are doing. Due to the novel subject, the emphasis is on explaining energy body dynamics. Supportive procedures and exercises are provided in the text as well as in the Appendix. For additional perspectives and exercises, you may also find value in two of my other books, penned as Ken Eagle Feather, *On the Toltec Path* and *Toltec Dreaming*.

Over millennia the Toltec investigators of perception have delivered a most sophisticated body of knowledge about the energy body, providing concrete, consistent references that detail the energy body as a well-defined, objective, and measurable part of our anatomy. Toltec theory also offers a unified perspective, a wider accounting of the knowledge gained in the various disciplines that study the world as energy. By its very nature, it includes the entire sphere of human activity and does so in a manner typically not outlined in the classic literature of other metaphysical systems.

The expanse of this perspective and the possibilities it highlights make this particular study of the human condition worth investigating. In a way, this is quite odd, as this highly refined worldview was developed some five thousand years ago in the innermost regions of what is now a third world country, Mexico. At the same time, what Toltec philosophy represents doesn't reside in a vacuum. From modern science to homeopathy to ancient Taoism, other fields, cultures, and individuals have contributed to our knowledge of the energy body. Studies of the energy body may rightly be relegated to many disciplines such as religious studies, anthropology, psychology, and physics.

Therefore, this work is based on a synthesis of Toltec perspectives with fields such as bioenergetics and transpersonal psychology, simultaneously revealing the structure and dynamics of the energy body and offering a context for a greater understanding of perception and personal growth. The overarching theme is that what goes on within the energy body is the principal determinant in all that we see, feel, think, or otherwise perceive. While the discussion is informed by the strength, vitality, and value of the ancient Toltec tradition, it also references various fields of inquiry that support and guide the basic premise.

"A World of Energy" offers an introduction to an arena where science and metaphysics blend, and where a shift in what we perceive as reality is occurring. As exemplified by His Holiness the Dalai Lama's book *The Universe of a Single Atom,* we are at a point in our evolution where the worlds of scientific and consciousness research are merging.[4]

"Anatomy of the Energy Body" outlines the components and perceptual abilities of our extended self. It also provides an overview of the mechanics relating to how our thoughts create the bits and pieces of the reality of our daily life and how our feelings hold this tapestry together. Applied to an individual or to a society, these reference points can help guide us to freedom or can unmercifully constrain us. To enable you to comprehend and command this process, "Constructing Reality" offers insights into how models of our world are developed. In "Expanding the Boundaries" energy body processes are related to various ways to adventure into other worlds and states of consciousness.

You may find that your beliefs are challenged every step of the way. Suspension of belief is at the heart of the scientific method, as well as Eastern mysticism, where the world is seen as an illusion, and in Toltec views where the world (any world) is considered to be just one of many real possibilities. This perceptual shift is the soul of objectivity. By learning to manage your beliefs, you can conceive of and even construct new orders of reality. In and of itself, this will renew and invigorate your life, which is why "Reflection and Projection" delves more deeply into how we form reality.

Some of the stultifying effects of our models of reality are then examined in "The Nature of Fundamentalism." "A Creative Life" provides perspectives to help you enhance your energy, as well as gain understanding of the intrinsic barriers to unfolding your awareness and the stages of growth you can anticipate. You will also find lessons on the blessings and dangers you may encounter wherever you venture.

"The Unfolding Moment" looks at the result of developing the energy body. It deals with the immediacy of life, where personal awareness intersects infinity. While this connection is ever-present, we are typically not conscious of it. Living this ongoing moment reflects quintessential human intelligence—ontological intelligence—and is usually described as the state of *being,* a state of fulfillment, awareness, and grace.

As mentioned, the Appendix, "Energy Management Skills,"

includes exercises that will guide your active exploration of the views presented. You may share the resulting experiences with others or they may be completely subjective. Either way, the material in the earlier chapters will give you the ability to make sense of them in a larger format of stimulating your energy body, adventuring in imagination, and accelerating your learning.

The purpose of this book, then, is to provide the context and means to enable you to enhance your cognitive skills of awareness and learning so that you may time and again revitalize your life, even redefining what that means. Realizing this quest rests on finding the energized moment of your energized reality.

1

A World of Energy

Throughout the course of your daily life, you live in the midst of infinity. In each moment, with each step, you have an infinite number of options at your beck and call. Consider the circle, which is defined as an infinite number of points that are connected—that is to say, a closed curve on a plane—with each point being the same distance from a fixed point, the center of the circle. Now, stand in the middle of a room. Keeping your feet in the same place (the center of the circle), rotate 360 degrees and end where you began. As you have created a circle, by definition you have the ability to access an infinite number of points or directions. You can also behave in an infinite number of ways. As though taking compass readings, from your starting point, any movement, small or large, will place you in a different space, a different orientation from where you started.

If you accept this, questions then arise regarding how you can navigate this immensity, how you can relate to it, how you can move with it, how you can expand your reference and relation to it, and how you can grow within it. The fact is that we typically limit our options, confining perception and behavior within a narrow slice of the possibilities. Breaking through these barriers is often a slow process. We need to find out how to relate to the vastness of life to continually awaken to new awareness, new knowledge.

In the history of human development, there have been defining moments during which group awareness has expanded and the world has been turned on its ear. These moments have often stretched over decades if not centuries, as new ways of looking at the world—such as viewing it as round instead of flat or revolving around the Sun rather than vice versa—have gradually found their way from idea to wide acceptance to established fact.

Indeed, our reality is "simply" a matter of perception, of organizing an immense number of bits of data into a coherent form that both awakens and limits our sense of the world. Like taking a compass reading, our orientation to life provides the parameters of what is considered to be possible. For someone who sees the world as flat, a voyage across the sea to distant lands is not possible, because it would mean falling to one's doom. So the attempt is not made. On the other hand, a worldview that incorporates within it the accurate movement of heavenly bodies allows for the possibility of safe navigation across oceans and even traveling to the moon and back. In the light of new perceptions daring souls accept the challenge to go beyond what others say just can't be.

We are living in such a defining moment of human history, a moment where the entire world, including us, is now seen as being made of energy. A quantum physicist will certainly tell you this, and be able to back up this claim with all the appropriate facts and figures. A laying-on-of-hands healer, an acupuncturist, or a homeopath is apt to tell you the same thing, albeit in different ways based on their training. A traditionally trained biologist or medical doctor who is now on the cutting edge of his or her discipline may also portray the world in such terms.

The ramifications of this shift in worldview are beyond current imagination. It will usher in new paradigms of psychology, health, ecology, business, and technology. Indeed, all areas of human endeavor will be transformed, as it will require a complete reassessment of actualities and potentials. The implications of this revised worldview for health and healing alone are staggering. A survey of the various aspects of the changes that will result from the recognition that we—and the world—are comprised first and foremost of energy is beyond the scope of this work. Instead, it focuses on the anatomy and general psychological mechanics of the energy body.

The energy-body model presented here not only represents a unifying umbrella for all bioenergetic modalities and technologies but also offers methods and means to address personal and group circumstances, including those of emotional and physical health. As part of our natural being, the energy body not only connects us with our daily world but determines the complete range of our perceptions and behavior. Thus a substantial reorientation of the energy body results in a foundational shift in reality. The emphasis on healing in this chapter shows the practical bottom-line potential of such inquiry.

BIOENERGETICS[1]

Bioenergy is at the root of a sweeping new field of inquiry, which suggests that the world is comprised of energy and that physical objects occur as a result of this energy. A branch of biophysics, the multidisciplinary field of study called *bioenergetics* is "the study of the flow and transformation of energy in and between living organisms and between living organisms and their environment."[2] As the term indicates, it deals with biology (the study of all life) and energy (perhaps the underlying substance of all life) and where these two intersect. The meeting area between biology and energy is immense, perhaps going beyond imagination. As virtually every area of human activity and every nook and cranny of our world is touched by bioenergy, it can form the basis of an entirely new cosmology.

The idea of energy playing a role within the body is well established within modern science. The root activity of the central nervous system is electrical and brain waves are measured by frequency. These days the elucidation of energy within the body is becoming even more enhanced. The specialty of biophysics evolved as a natural result of physicists furthering their research into all areas where energy plays a role. This discipline has grown to include topics such as cellular communication, neurobiology, and the role of photons and electrons within the human body.

As a result of these types of investigation, we are rapidly increasing our appreciation of the fact that energy fields cause a wide variety of physical occurrences. In his landmark text, *Energy Medicine: The Scientific Basis*, biophysicist James Oschman points out that the resonant properties of DNA have already been documented, as has DNA's response to pulsing magnetic fields. He also describes an extracellular matrix found throughout the body and its multifaceted relation to energy fields. This matrix "exerts specific and important influences upon cellular dynamics, just as much as hormones and neurotransmitters."[3]

In addition, the new field of energy psychology explores models of how the psyche works at an energetic level and, based on this, practitioners are developing therapies that significantly speed recovery. At the same time the world of technology is ushering in devices that are revealing and altering biologic energy fields, and even interacting with the matrix of universal energy.

Without necessarily being called such, bioenergetics has deep historical roots. As part of traditional Chinese medicine (TCM), acupuncture has been practiced for at least two thousand years. At the heart of acupuncture are meridians, channels that create an energetic circuit throughout the body. This flow is not unlike the movement of blood through the circulatory system, which requires proper regulation for health. Meridians are also the biological connection with the notion of *qi,* or life energy.[4] Needles are inserted into the skin along the channel routes to restore and regulate the natural flow of energy. Since acupuncture is performed with minimal invasiveness, adverse side effects are also minimal—an important consideration given the toll that the side effects of pharmaceuticals often produce.

Chakras are described as forming yet another energetic circuit within the body. In a basic view, chakras are energy centers occurring along the length of the spine, each accounting for a different mode of perception. The root chakra at the base of the spine, for instance, is typically viewed as relating to physicality, whereas the crown chakra located at the top of the head relates to spiritual orientation. Many laying-on-of-hands practices, such as Reiki work, lie within the chakra framework, which was developed in Eastern cultures.[5]

A more recent model of energetic healing is found in homeopathy. In 1810, its inventor, physician Samuel Hahnemann, published the formative treatise, *Organon of the Medical Art,* in which he detailed the practice of using small amounts of a substance that corresponds to a disease to treat it, a "like cures like" principle. In addition, through *succussing,* during which the solution is vigorously shaken, as well as repeatedly diluting the solution, the physical molecules are gradually removed until only an energetic trace remains, establishing another principle of "less is more." According to Hahnemann, this *potentizes* the formulation, which acts directly on the "vital force," the underlying essential energy of the patient. This, in turn, causes the physical body to respond and heal.[6]

Homeopathy is credited with reducing the suffering experienced during the infectious disease plagues that swept Europe during the 1800s. Toward the end of that century, as the scientific models of biology and chemistry gained popularity, homeopathy began to be viewed by many as quackery. Reflecting a revival of interest in the United States, however, the National Center for Complementary and Alternative Medicine (NCCAM), part of the National Institutes of Health, is now providing grants for scientific evaluation of homeopathy. In Europe the practice of homeopathy is returning to its earlier popularity, typified by such centers as the Paracelsus Clinic in Lustmuhle, Switzerland, which uses homeopathy as a core approach in treating cancer and other illnesses from a *biological medicine* perspective.[7]

In the early 1900s, Royal Rife discovered cancer virus, an accomplishment not verified by medical science until the late 1950s. He went on to find a specific electromagnetic frequency that, when targeted at cancer cells, caused their destruction, setting the stage for later considerations that every organism has its own electromagnetic signature or a waveform associated with its genetic makeup. Rife's work was considered controversial, to say the least, with many agencies working to suppress it, but today it remains a focus of active reference within the field of bioenergetics.[8]

A principal, and most compelling, feature separating many of these therapies from the allopathic biomedical model is that bioenergy-based modes of healing often require an examination of the total person and view illness as an expression of disharmony both internally and externally. Treatment in the Western allopathic model, on the other hand, is intended to antagonize the disease, which is seen as something separate from the patient. Often symptoms alone are attacked, causing harmful side effects, whereas in holistic models adverse side effects are purposefully minimized if not eliminated. I'm not arguing that one perspective is better than the other, as I think both models have value according to the situation. While it is an interesting debate, a full-blown discussion is well outside the scope of this work.

As Clark Manning and Louis Vanrenen, authors of *Bioenergetic Medicines East and West,* point out, one of the difficulties for a new field such as this is the lack of instrumentation to adequately measure effects and results.[9] Scientific tools to measure chakras, meridians, and such energy systems have been slow to develop since these avenues of energy haven't found widespread acceptance in scientific thought. Chakras remain on the fringes of simple mention, let alone rigorous study. At the same time, scientists are accumulating extensive data relating to different energetic processes such as cellular metabolism and communication.

Modern physics is also addressing this problem of a lack of instrumentation. At the leading edge of this type of innovation is the SQUID (superconducting quantum interference device) magnetometer, a highly sensitive technology that can map biomagnetic fields produced by physiological processes within the body. Its development was spear-headed by J. E. Zimmerman, who was once a Ford Motor Company scientist. SQUID was the first practical electronic instrument to detect interference between the energy waves of matter and is currently considered one of the best detectors of magnetic flux. In conjunction with SQUID technology, special rooms to shield environmental energies have recently been built to study extremely subtle magnetic fields of the brain and other areas of the body.[10]

Another invention comes from Konstantin Korotkov, a physics professor at Russia's St. Petersburg State Technical University. An expert in the field of bioelectrography, Korotkov developed a computerized device that permits what he refers to as Gas Discharge Visualization (GDV). Based on Kirlian photography, the GDV allows the observation of human energy fields, and so can help in observing the changes in energy in a variety of situations, including when therapies are administered.[11]

Still another emerging technology with great promise for diagnosing physical and mental disease is Polycontrast Interference Photography (PIP). Invented by British researcher Harry Oldfield, it consists of a digital camera and proprietary software that tracks the energy emitted when two waveforms intersect. The resulting photonic discharge provides a picture that illuminates areas of disease and health. Chakras, meridians, and physiologic states are easily discernible, as is the effect of environmental influences and intention. Oldfield has been collaborating in the United States with physician Brian Dailey and in India with investigator Thornton Streeter, Director of the Centre for Biofield Sciences. In one study the crown chakra of a person diagnosed as psychotic was clearly split. In another profile, PIP mapped an experienced meditator's shifts as he went from normal waking consciousness into deep meditation and back to waking.[12]

Many effective medical and healing disciplines, both established and emerging, are aspects of bioenergetics. If healing practices and related hardwired technologies—which cut to the core of the human condition—are an effect of energy and require looking at the entire person, then the quantum physicist's "unified field" and the mystic's experience that "all is one" come together to portray a common world. This brings us closer to the universal components, to the common denominators, of the human experience regardless of race, gender, or creed.

Initially, the term bioenergetics was defined as "a form of psychology based on the use of kinesthetics and muscle testing to assess energy flow and levels," so the field is rooted in physical anatomy. Physician Alexander Lowen popularized it with his book *Bioenergetics*.[13] More recently, in his book *Energy Psychology,* psychologist Fred Gallo shows how the discipline has grown by revealing connections between cognition, energy, and behavior, and placing the movement and blockages of energy squarely in the center of why disorders manifest.[14]

Bioenergetics is also now defined as the study of metabolic activity at the cellular level. Based on this orientation, scientists at leading universities are demonstrating the role of energetic flow and transformation in disease and healing. The University of Colorado's Institute of Bioenergetics at Colorado Springs, for example, is building "a multidisciplinary approach to understanding cellular metabolism and cellular communication with the intention of treating or curing serious diseases."[15] The area of cellular signaling (how cells communicate) is also evolving from the study of physical processes—such as a hormone docking with a receptor, which in turn sets a cascade of events into motion—to investigating energetic signaling where the "first cause" of the physical cascade is energetic in nature.

Another area of investigation is unfolding in the laboratory of John McMichael, immunologist, virologist, and founder of Beech Tree Labs and the Institute for Therapeutic Discovery.[16] Decades of research in the laboratory and in preclinical studies have shown the value of a class of formulations that use low levels of naturally occurring molecules to address a wide spectrum of disorders. The dosages are far above those used in homeopathy but far lower than those used in current pharmaceuticals, and so point the way to an entirely new platform for looking at how the body works.

After McMichael's novel therapy for depression demonstrated efficacy, scientists at the University of North Carolina at Chapel Hill also discovered that it didn't act through the biopathways typically associated with modern antidepressants. These findings produced speculation that the agent might work through a form of energetic communication that tells the body to restore balance. McMichael himself holds open the possibility that there may be an energetic circuit comprised of receptors in cells or in the extracellular matrix that plays a role in the restoration of homeodynamics (a more descriptive term for "homeostasis"), the body's natural harmony.

Also on the cutting edge of bioenergetics is "nonlocal" healing where the well-focused *intent* of an individual or a group may significantly affect the health of someone thousands of miles away. While this practice is often placed in a spiritual or religious category, the mechanism of nonlocal healing is usually viewed as energy related, whether it is focused through dowsing, prayer, or other means. Among those who are scientifically examining the mechanism by which such healing occurs are physician Larry Dossey and research scientist Marilyn Mandala Schlitz of the Institute of Noetic Sciences, with promising, albeit inconsistent, results.[17] Intentionality is often thought to be the common denominator of how the various approaches to nonlocal healing focus energy.

In nonscientific terms, there has been an enormous amount of research on the energetics of living systems. In the past this research has simply not been viewed in the context of Western cultural practices and concepts. This is changing. Science is beginning to catch up to what Toltecs have been saying about the world, and to the healing practices TCM has been offering the world for centuries. It seems obvious, then, that the healing therapies of bioenergetics—often referred to as "energy medicine"—are quite diverse, have deep historical roots, and comprise an emerging multidisciplinary arena in the modern world of science.

If energy is in any way a determinant for biological actions and reactions, then new models, new variables for study, and new technologies for healing and wellness will continue to sprout. At the same time, these revelations are not casting an entirely new net of awareness over the scientific world. They are based on preceding knowledge. "The emerging concepts do not require us to abandon our sophisticated understandings of physiology, biochemistry, or molecular biology," maintains Oschman. "Instead they extend our picture of living processes, and of healing, to finer levels of structure and function."[18]

The human body constantly receives and emits magnetic electrical information or other types of energy-based signals. From taking in the Sun's energy and converting it to vitamin D, to sound affecting regions of the brain, to receptors in the eye that detect photons, the body has an array of energy-detection apparatuses. Chemical reactions, characteristic of a biochemical model of the body, occur due to the burst of energy caused by the stimulation. Furthermore, there are over a hundred years of research behind the modern field of electromyography, the tracking of electrical currents behind muscle movement, which shows this type of activity occurs naturally within the body.[19]

Oschman, a recognized leader in the field of biophysics, says, "We are in a period of dramatic change in the healthcare system. Energy Medicine has a huge role to play in this process. The reason is that conventional Western medicine is the only medical system in history that has virtually ignored energetics. Energetic concepts are part of nearly all of the complementary and alternative therapies that the public is enthusiastically moving toward." Quoting Albert Szent-Györgyi (who won a Nobel Prize in 1937 for his synthesis of vitamin C), Oschman continues, "'In every culture and in every medical tradition before ours, healing was accomplished by moving energy.'"[20]

As physicist Milo Wolff points out, "Nothing happens in nature without an energy exchange. Communication or acquisition of knowledge of any kind occurs only with an energetic transfer. There are no exceptions. This is a rule of nature."[21]

TRANSPERSONAL PSYCHOLOGY

The blossoming field of energy psychology is an aspect of bioenergetics as well as that of transpersonal psychology. The Institute of Transpersonal Psychology defines this discipline as "the extension of psychological studies into consciousness studies, spiritual inquiry, body-mind relationships, and transformation." As such, it deals with the breadth and depth of perception and behavior. It is the fourth force of psychology, with behaviorism, psychoanalysis, and humanism being the others. The first three are often associated with B. F. Skinner, Sigmund Freud, and Abraham Maslow, respectively. Yet Maslow would later become dissatisfied with just a humanistic approach. As signaled by the first publication of *The Journal of Transpersonal Psychology* in 1969, a group of psychologists including Maslow, Anthony Sutich, and Charles T. Tart ushered in the fourth force.[22]

Traditional practices found in Zen Buddhism, Taoism, esoteric Christianity, and the Toltec Way are integral to transpersonal psychology. Indeed, Taoist teachings embody energy within a general worldview as well as meridians. Each of these systems also offers practices of meditation, personal growth, and ways to consciously evolve beyond the mortal plane. Plus, from the various works of such nineteenth-century theosophists as C. W. Leadbeater and Madame Helena Blavatsky to the more modern writings of Barbara Brennan, Valerie V. Hunt, and Fritjof Capra, the literature on aspects of the energy body continues to grow.

To date, religion and metaphysical philosophy have carried the banner of researching and explaining such things as the *mystical experience* where a person's consciousness expands well beyond normal limits and a profound oneness with all creation is directly experienced. The advent of a new division of psychology allows for the secularization of this study and is already providing common cross-cultural definitions to further define it.

In addition, there is currently a strong movement to develop a science of consciousness. There are several quality books on this field, which is using rigorous scientific skills to examine what has been in the province of what some consider the soft sciences, such as psychology. Some of the most significant work has come from MIT Press, which has published a series appropriately titled *Toward a Science of Consciousness.*[23] This series stems from discussions and debates at the University of Arizona, that have brought together experts in fields such as philosophy, cognitive science, psychology, and physics.

From a wide-angle perspective, transpersonal psychology may be especially important, as it provides meaning pertaining to experiences beyond the currently accepted norms of daily human consciousness, including those of social consensus reality. In other words, it provides a telescope to examine the entire human experience and so enable us to look at how things are shaping up from an entirely different vantage point. It also reflects *positive psychology,* an area that Maslow has referred to as the psychology of the future, which deals with healthy, fully functioning people.[24] In contrast to *abnormal psychology*—the study of dysfunctions—which has received the preponderance of attention, positive psychology examines the brighter side of human development, including such things as hope, happiness, and healing.[25]

While transpersonal psychology brings academic and scientific rigor to investigations of consciousness, the greater body of it currently presents intellectual perspectives, which help set the stage for new navigational charts. This may change. Indeed, the combination of bio-energetic perspectives with a branch of psychology that examines consciousness may well enable us to develop a sophisticated model of states of dysfunction and their remedy. A practical effect of this work will be that the entire field of healing will change, if not explode into new directions.

TOLTEC THEORY

This background demonstrates that an energy-based perspective of reality doesn't exist on the fringes of speculation; rather, the study of the energy body already has a place within established fields. At the same time it must be underscored that while these contemporary fields are duly investigating aspects of energy, it is the centuries of efforts of metaphysical investigators from cultures around the world that have provided the framework for a modern scientific examination of the energy body. By its very nature, for example, the energy body is a model that accounts for all states of consciousness, including those of healing, personal transformation, and cosmology.

Toltec theory is psychological, as it deals first and foremost with perception. Backing this up, it details a structure of the energy body with all the elements that transform sensation into perception and then meaning. In great measure, Carlos Castaneda's body of work set the tone for subsequent Toltec literature because his books presented the essential framework of this metaphysical system.[26] In so doing, he standardized much of the terminology in a manner similar to any other academic, scientific, or trade discipline.

Mathematicians, biologists, or electricians, for instance, rely on common terms so that practitioners within the respective field from around the world may effectively communicate. The authors of contemporary Toltec books have similarly adopted much of the same terminology in their books, even though their individual relationships to the Toltec Way vary. I have also adopted some of this terminology describing the energy body, while modifying some terms to provide a more descriptive or practical viewpoint. Most of the current Toltec literature retains the flavor and terminology of days long past. In many ways, this is well and good, but the philosophy has so much to offer—not just for its adherents—that it deserves to be recast into more modern perspectives, a task very much in keeping with its teachings.

AN UPDATED HUMAN ANATOMY

The Toltecs established a view of extended, universal human anatomy, as well as a schema that demonstrates how its components and systems influence perception. Thus Toltec theory represents far more than a philosophical approach, as vital as that discipline is. Energy body anatomy also provides the objective reference needed to enable hard science skills to be employed in investigations that are not based on philosophical propositions, but on empirical measurements.

The energy body as a whole has four main components: *uniformity,* or its shape; *cohesion,* which reflects the overall coherence of energies within it; the *focal point,* which provides a reference to the type of cohesion; and *core,* the innermost area of the energy body, the cool spot of the flame, our direct connection with infinity itself.[27]

Various dimensions of awareness reside within the energy body. The physical body is one segment of the energy body. It is experienced when cohesion is stabilized in a certain way. If you shift cohesion just a little you might experience a change of mood or have different thoughts. If you shift it more so, and thereby reform cohesion to a greater extent, it is possible to experience other dimensions of reality or perceive the world from completely different perspectives, such as in an out-of-body experience.

As cohesion is the container that holds the various energies of the individual, one of its primary determinants is uniformity. Each member of the human species has a similar uniformity, as do other species. This shape changes over time, which may eventually provide a useful perspective on evolution, since a change of shape changes cohesion, which then causes new perceptions, new physical attributes, and new behaviors.

The focal point offers a reference for what type of cohesion has been formed. The focal point of a person having a strong intellectual bent will be positioned in a certain area, while the focal point of a nervous or unstable person will wiggle about, not being able to rest or stabilize in a specific position.

A mental disorder or physical disease is marked by one position, health by another. A specific disease is evidenced by the focal point being in a position corresponding to the particular disease. Whether a

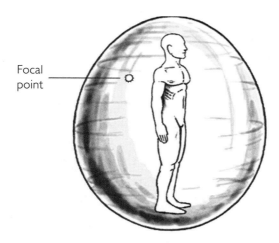

Focal point

Figure 1.1. The Energy Body
The energy body has a definitive form, but not a hardened boundary.

treatment is a homeopathic remedy, acupuncture, Reiki, or a scientific medical technology, in terms of Toltec theory, the mechanism by which the therapy works is the same. That is to say, the energy of the healing modality affects the energy of the person, thereby altering coherence. An effective therapy builds on this and actually changes the person's overall cohesion, which is reflected by a movement of the focal point. A shaman is one who has learned how to shift a person's focal point back to the "health" position by utilizing a range of procedures, which typically are based on a view of the world as being comprised of energy, perhaps using the word "spirit" in lieu of "energy."

Given that cohesion and the focal point are not part of traditional medical training, a physician approaches healing from quite a different vantage point. From an energy body perspective, however, both shaman and doctor have the same effect, that of shifting the focal point. No matter the technique, then, the concept that all perceptions and states of being are derived from the mechanics of the energy body is a basic premise of this book. This applies to each and every person walking the earth. This knowledge alone could create entirely new and varied industries of research, education, and technology.

TWO SIDES, THREE FIELDS

A friend once remarked to me, "There are two types of people: those who separate everything into two and those who don't."

Knowing the two sides of the energy body is fundamental to understanding its structure and use. Simply, they are the right and left sides. In terms of bioenergetics, they are the *first* and *second energy fields*. In terms of psychology, they are the *conscious* and *unconscious* parts of your awareness. *Learning* and *imagination*—which respectively emphasize stability and rapid expansion of awareness—are the two fundamental, integral approaches to develop both sides of the energy body.[28]

Developing the two sides may lead to awareness of a *third energy field,* a dimension that exists outside the energy body yet impacts it as it puts pressure on the energy body, giving it shape and substance. A key aspect of this field is the emanations of energy arising from a single source, the source of all creation. These are packages or streams of awareness that have a powerful influence on the shape of the energy body and what occurs within it, thereby determining the focal point position. As such, this falls neatly within the definition of bioenergetics, as the flow and transformation of energy between the energy body and the environment is taken into consideration.

This third field can also be understood as the *supraconscious*, a domain of awareness that contains the other two fields, yet is far vaster. Cultivating awareness of the third field is the line of demarcation between the ancient and modern Toltecs. Moreover, doing so eventually removes you from the art and craft of Toltec practices and places you in a more sublime arena, that of the *self-actualized* person, someone who has achieved a fundamental transformation in his or her energy body by activating the full range of innate abilities.

While Maslow put forth *self-actualization* as the capstone of psychological development, C. G. Jung regarded this as *individuation*. In essence, both approaches pertain to becoming more human as governed by a natural order of how one is created rather than by the definitions and confinement of human-made order. Although I don't think either had the energy body in mind, in principle there is no disparity, despite differences in terminology; all of these viewpoints deal with fulfilled, complete, psychologically healthy people. That there can be common denominators among established lines of thought only serves to demonstrate the viability of continued investigation concerning what it means and what it takes to achieve this level. In fact, the founders of transpersonal psychology have suggested that the study of actualization should be a new branch of psychology called *ontopsychology,* a hybrid term incorporating ontology and psychology.[29]

Ontology can be defined in many ways. Here it refers to a central part of metaphysics that deals with the study of *being,* with the essence of a thing. Metaphysics relates to the time-honored philosophical traditions that are concerned with the essential nature of reality, reality formation, and the underlying principles of the universe.[30] Transpersonal psychologies and some energy-based psychologies would find a natural place within this field. The energy-body model of consciousness serves the development of ontopsychology, providing objective references as well as schematics regarding how to become self-actualized or individuated.

Regardless of its divisions, branches, or schools of thought, psychology is still psychology. If we use the root derivation of the term, it is "the study of mind."[31] Perhaps the energy body as a whole is what philosophers call "mind" and at the core of it resides what theologians call "soul." And perhaps the two sides also relate to the left and right hemispheres of the brain, while the three fields relate to the vertical partitioning of the brain into the reptilian, paleomammilian, and neo-mammilian sections.[32] In other words, in days to come this extended bioenergetic anatomy could provide a more in-depth basis for philosophical, physiological, and other perspectives.

SELF-REFLECTION

Modern Toltecs focus on the unrelenting quest to awaken their entire energy bodies as a means to engage the third field, not to mention for the sheer adventure of doing so. But you don't have to be a Toltec to embark on such a voyage. Anyone can set his or her mind to it. The principal way to facilitate this journey is to manage *self-reflection,* the almost constant mental and emotional form of referencing that we engage in about ourselves, others, and our world. When management of self-reflection is combined with stopping our thoughts, the flow of our mental energy, it will deliver a one-two punch that knocks out the images of our preconceived world. All other perspectives and procedures are secondary to this challenge.[33]

No matter what the scheme of things—flat earth, shamanism, bioenergetics, or otherwise—the idea is that the world we perceive is based on interlocking thoughts that form a grand composite. What we think the world is becomes a self-fulfilling prophecy where we verify our own thoughts day in and day out. The trick, then, is to stop thinking . . . at least long enough, and regularly enough, to allow new perceptions to enter into our conscious world, to allow new thoughts to form, and then to repeat this time and again. It is therefore a means of discovering what exists, not what we think exists.

A NEW FIELD OF INQUIRY

Most current bioenergetic methods address physical health and healing. Only when we bring in certain areas of physics does this expand to an entire worldview based on energy. Even then, our knowledge is limited as to the range of bioenergetic circuits in the body and environment. By updating human anatomy, we vastly expand the scope of bioenergetics. We can apply the structure, function, and processes of the energy body to virtually any endeavor. Understanding how uniformity, cohesion, perception, and experience interact would affect the practice of medicine, all forms and schools of psychology, ecology, and technology.

As presented here, all of the pieces for this already exist. The foundation of this enterprise consists of

- a cosmological environment that is comprised of energy, as detailed by physics and Toltec shamanism
- the anatomy of the individual energy body, including the functions of its parts and systems, as outlined by scientific and metaphysical disciplines
- the processes to facilitate and guide these interactions, as provided by several psychological models, with applications ranging from the abnormal to the positive
- the core discipline of bioenergetics examining all aspects of the flow and exchange of energy from individual and environmental perspectives, which brings it full circle

Relating this to consciousness studies yields the multidisciplinary field of *transpersonal bioenergetics*, in which the enduring, highly valuable work of an indigenous tradition is made accessible to everyone through the integration of its universal perspectives with the best knowledge from a variety of ancient and contemporary fields. The results of applying these perspectives to your life could be quite astonishing.

A NEW WORLD

The chapters to come offer you ways to look at and feel the world around you, to take stock of yourself as you learn what you are made of, as well as discover processes of exploring uncharted territories and determining the directions of your life.

This is a never-ending journey. If you stop learning, crashing is inevitable, rapid entropy assured. If you continue, be prepared for transformations of many kinds, as you leave your known world behind, bit-by-bit, then leap-by-leap.

All said and done, the beckoning of awareness is all you have. Eventually it will take you past all known channel markers, beyond all current models. This book offers you ways and means to embark on a journey that will take you beyond your known world and deliver you to the infinity that is within and without, residing right here, right now, no matter what you are doing. There you have it: a new world, one that has been before you all along. The objective is to awaken your energy body to its fullest capacity to live a full and conscious life. What happens along the way is up to you.

2
Anatomy of the Energy Body

An energized world is reality. We live in a world driven, consumed, and managed by energy. From the sun's rays to wind to batteries to medical technologies, virtually nothing in our lives escapes the domain of energy.

It is also clear that this reality is being continually revealed and applied. In simple illustrations, engineers are learning how to better harness sun and wind power, physicists now deal with scalar and vector energies and measurements (a vector is linear and finite, whereas scalar energies emanate instantaneously everywhere), and medical scientists have demonstrated that pulsed magnetic therapy has value for healing bone fractures.[1] By definition, all of these applications fit into a bioenergetic view of our world. Keeping this in mind, it is less of a stretch to view human anatomy as being comprised of energy.

We typically view the world as made up of material, solid objects. Perceiving the world as external objects hinges on the agreements we collectively make about the world, agreements that have been handed down unchallenged for centuries. As a result, we have produced a world based on a collection of assumptions *about* reality. In other words, we have inherited a description of reality so powerful that we have validated it time and time again without ever having learned to step beyond it.

The multidisciplinary approach of bioenergetics offers a fresh option: a universe comprised of energy. As with any theory, it's possible to make an extensive categorization of various types of energy and their effects. If we hold that the world is energy, then each person, place, and thing in the world is energy. And each group of items, such as humans, trees, or clouds, has its own energetic dynamics. Then there is another set of processes for how they interact. The more you are able to recognize these dynamics, the more you will become aware of yourself, your circumstances, and your growth.

To enhance such an exploration, you need to know the mechanical structure and capabilities of your conveyance, just as it is important to know that if you want to travel three thousand miles in one day, an automobile isn't the best vehicle. In like manner, flying a small propeller-driven plane requires different skills than flying a jet airliner. And not knowing how to use the rigging of a sailboat during a storm leads to major trouble. In each case, knowing the nature of the craft—its capacities, its structure and layout, and how it functions in part and in whole—provides for a better journey.

Here, the craft is the energy body. Even the physical body is considered by Toltecs to be an effect of the energy body, one option of human awareness. Human anatomy is thus far greater than what is usually understood. The following exploration of various aspects of energetic anatomy, such as the central nervous system, as well as other physical-body systems like the chakras, will provide a better sense of this extended perspective. That will prepare us to enter more fully into Toltec-based theory and examine the major components of uniformity, cohesion, focal point, and core. All the while you need to understand that we are reviewing the structure of the universe of energy to help us connect with and perceive it, just as the physical models of planets, solar systems, and galaxies enable us to better perceive the physical cosmos.

PHYSICAL-BODY ENERGY SYSTEMS

An overriding consideration is that there is already an established framework for understanding human perception and behavior as described and measured in terms of energy. There is acceptance of and scientific research on energetic aspects of human anatomy, such as the nervous system, brain waves, and acupuncture meridians. Awareness of the aspects of an energy body and the energy body itself can then be regarded as an extension of what is already known. The aspects mentioned here by no means represent a complete list of what researchers around the world are tackling. But a brief review will make the point about the viability of an energy-based model of humans.

The Nervous System

The human nervous system is principally divided into central and peripheral parts. The *central nervous system* consists of the brain and spinal cord. It performs an array of functions, from processing information to generating reflexes to higher cognitive functions. The *peripheral system* connects the central nervous system with both outer and inner environments; it is further divided into sensory and motor functions. Sensory functions, including taste, touch, sight, and so on, regulate the various forms of environmental energies that affect the body, while motor functions relate to body movements such as intentionally turning the pages of a book.[2]

The *autonomic system* is the central watchdog of all internal neural functions and is further divided into the *sympathetic* and *parasympathetic systems*. These systems work together; for example, the sympathetic system tightens the gastrointestinal sphincters and the parasympathetic system loosens them.

Communication within the nervous system is performed by cells called *neurons*. This communication is typically studied in terms of electrical energy, such as "action potential" and "states of excitation" that describe aspects of the movement of electrical signals and information along the same neural pathways that also convey chemical substances.

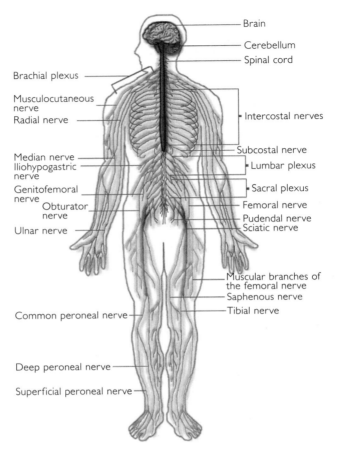

Brain
Cerebellum
Spinal cord
Brachial plexus
Musculocutaneous nerve
Radial nerve
Intercostal nerves
Median nerve
Iliohypogastric nerve
Genitofemoral nerve
Obturator nerve
Ulnar nerve
Subcostal nerve
Lumbar plexus
Sacral plexus
Femoral nerve
Pudendal nerve
Sciatic nerve
Muscular branches of the femoral nerve
Saphenous nerve
Tibial nerve
Common peroneal nerve
Deep peroneal nerve
Superficial peroneal nerve

Figure 2.1. Nervous System
(Illustration courtesy of Wikimedia Commons)

Brain Waves

One of the ways to discern brain behavior is by measuring electrical energy. The electroencephalograph (EEG) provides an indication of states of consciousness by registering activity associated with several bands of brain-wave frequencies measured in hertz (Hz) or cycles per second. Different studies may list different frequencies; however, they usually vary only within a range of .5–1 Hz. One researcher provides a schematic of brain-wave frequencies as consisting of delta (.5–3 Hz), theta (4–7 Hz), alpha (8–12 Hz), beta (14–30 Hz), and gamma (30–50 Hz). Dominance of any band often indicates a certain state of awareness, such as relaxation, mental activity, agitation, reverie, various stages of sleep, and even peak athletic performance. An EEG pattern thereby provides a map, or at least a sense of what a subject is experiencing.[3]

Other Physical Systems

Stemming from the work of physician Robert Becker, author of *The Body Electric,* Oschman has described a *perineural system* consisting of the connective tissue surrounding the nervous system.[4] Controlling the repair of injury, it acts in a more wide-reaching capacity with expansive nonlinear properties, while the nervous system is linear, directing information and activity along specific lines.

In addition, biophysicists, engineers, medical doctors, educators, and other like-minded professionals have formed an alliance to study *biologic closed electrical circuits.* Members focus on the use of a variety of energy-based therapies—electrical, magnetic, thermal—to treat an array of diseases. Their work is based on the idea that there are circulating, self-regulating loops of energy within the body that use a number of physiologic pathways and functions for healing.[5]

Meridians and Acupuncture

Referring to acupuncture as a medical science, the World Health Organization has classified fourteen meridians with 361 classical acupuncture points.[6] Traditional Chinese medicine (TCM), of which acupuncture is a part, deals with recognizing and treating disharmony among the various elements of the body that have been singled out as important over thousands of years of research.

Fundamental textures of qi, blood, essence, spirit, and fluids—along with their individual and collective effect on homeodynamics—are all taken into account. Each texture has several aspects. Qi has positive and negative functions relating to nutrition, protection, deficiencies, and stagnation. Blood is the yin-yang opposite of qi. Whereas

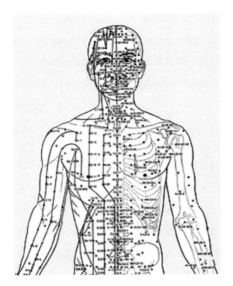

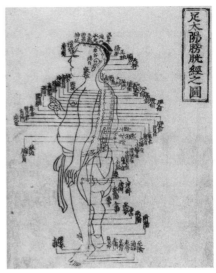

Figure 2.2a. Meridians

Acupuncture, simply put, involves the manipulation of meridians—the channels of qi—to help restore harmony throughout the body. Charts like the one above serve to guide the placement of acupuncture needles. (This illustration is used with the kind permission of Devatara J. Holman, Marin Oriental Medicine, Sausalito, California, www.marinorientalmedicine.com.)

Figure 2.2b. Acupuncture chart from Hua Shou
(fl. 1340s, Ming Dynasty)

This illustration is from *Shi si jing fa hui (Expression of the Fourteen Meridians)* Tokyo, Suharaya Heisuke kanko, Kyoho gan, 1716. (Illustration courtesy of Wikimedia Commons)

qi energizes, blood relaxes. Essence relates to the intrinsic nature separating animate and inanimate worlds, and spirit is the defining quality of humanness. The fluids of the body nourish and moisten.[7]

A refinement of worldview and practice is added when the textures are viewed in relation to organs, another principal part of TCM. The liver, for instance, is connected with blood as well as tempering qi. The kidneys, in turn, are the foundation upon which water or fluids may work with the rest of the body.[8]

Chakras

Chakras are energy generators, each associated with a specific function. Traditionally, there are seven energy centers comprising the chakra system. These are located in proximity to the spinal column and ascend from the base of the spine to the crown of the head. Some research presents the chakra system as a nonphysical loop of energy entering the bottoms of the feet, traversing upward, leaving the top of the head, and flowing outward and back down. Some investigations portray the chakras as having physical correlates with specific organs, often those of the endocrine glandular system, while other investigations relegate them more to general locations not necessarily directly associated with organs. Invariably, though, chakras are seen as affecting the physical body as well as connecting the physical body to physical and nonphysical environments inside and outside the energy body.

Each chakra has a vibration. The higher along the spine a chakra is located, the higher its frequency. Thus chakras extend from the base level of red through the physical light spectrum to violet. So within your body you have a personal rainbow, the shade of which varies according to the person. These centers, combined with additional vertical channels of opposite polarity, are often referred to as

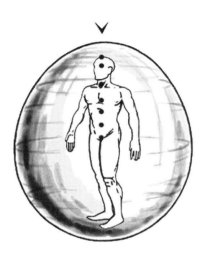

Figure 2.3. Chakras
   This is one
   representation of
   chakra locations.
   The "V" represents
   environmental
   influences.

the *kundalini system* or *tract*.[9] They may also be thought of as individual dimensions, or planes of awareness. Working with these dimensions helps you achieve a more powerful relationship with your entire energy body and your life.

Some systems present as many as thirteen chakras, with additional chakras located at the knees, ankles, the top and bottom of the energy body, as well as between the top of the head and the top of the energy body and between the bottoms of the feet and the bottom of the energy body. Combined, they produce the range or bandwidth of human perception. Different systems also ascribe different meanings for each chakra. The following model is fairly generic. The idea behind it is not to provide a detailed map, but a simple schematic to offer a sense of the different aspects of our being.

Location	Color	Perception
Base of spine	Red	This energy pertains to the physical world.
Abdomen	Orange	Here we find emotional energy. Some systems place sexual energy here; other systems place sexual energy in the first center.
Solar plexus	Yellow	Mental or intellectual energy. The beginning of the power of discrimination, of making refined distinctions.
Heart	Green	This energy provides for our connection with the world outside of our personal self. We begin to feel unity with the world.
Base of throat	Light blue	Communication energy. Also, this is often regarded as the entrance into more abstract regions of awareness, perhaps the initial realization of God.
Forehead	Dark blue	Psychic energy, often referred to as the *third eye*. Some metaphysical systems regard this as *will*.
Crown of the head	Violet	Spiritual dimensions. The link between the personal self and more-than-human regions.

To further elaborate:

Red, at the base of the spine. This is raw power, the baseline for physical-body and physical-world manifestations. Life as we know it is an immediate extension of this primal world. Some energy exercises focus on this root chakra to explosively release energy through the entire kundalini system, pushing awareness deep into unrealized territory.

The first chakra is often considered the densest of energies. It may be the densest within the ordinary human experience, but there are denser energies in the cosmos. Esoteric and scientific literature detail regions of immense density, far outstripping the normal physical world we experience.

Orange, at the abdomen. This chakra relates to emotions and is associated with the feeling cornerstone in Toltec theory. As it is the energy of emotion, it directly relates to dreaming or imagination. Where red is the wellspring of the physical world; orange is the wellspring of the dreaming, creative world.

Yellow, at the solar plexus. This is the energy of discernment, of discovering and classifying. As the chakras represent dimensions of awareness, the first, second, and third chakras build a three-dimensional world. Wanting to control your environment is the downside of the third chakra. You have such a sense of control, it's hard to let go to experience more . . . such as the fourth dimensional energies of the heart.

Green, at the heart. This energy enhances feeling. By developing it, you perceive subtleties, nuances, and refinements. The trick is to get out of yourself long enough to sense them. The fourth chakra opens you to worlds beyond yourself. And yet these worlds are also you.

The first three chakras represent the personal self: the physical, emotional, and mental aspects of separate, individual awareness. These energies have to be groomed to find your sense of self. From this point, you may enter worlds beyond your exclusive personal dimensions. Therefore the fourth chakra takes you into, and connects you with, your environment. The more you activate the fourth chakra, the more you balance with and feel part of the world, not a three-dimensional object separate from it.

Light blue, at the base of the throat. This is a curious energy, which deals with verbal communication. Charismatic people tend to have good control of this energy, and their voices are often mesmerizing. Whereas the fourth chakra opens you to your environment, this energy begins to connect you with an out-of-this world environment. Elevating your perception of the environment, you begin to step outside of the physical world and into nonphysical dimensions. For this reason, it is sometimes considered the entrance into God realization.

Dark blue, at the third eye. Tapping this energy gives you entrance into psychic functioning. You may experience visions, telepathy, or precognition. Becoming psychic means you have greater ability to work with nonphysical energies. However, this often results in getting stuck. You have power and don't want to let it go. To become actualized, however, you must manage the energies of the entire spectrum.

Violet, at the crown of the head. Whereas the first three chakras represent the personal self and the second set of three represent your environment, the seventh chakra is your entrance into worlds beyond the normal human domain. You enter heavenly dimensions of bliss and have mystical experiences. Since the energy is of a higher vibration, it translates to the physical body as ecstasy. It is for this reason that it is often considered the spiritual chakra.

Some people place additional chakras at different areas of the physical or energy bodies. For example, the palms of the hands as well as other areas of the body are often seen as having chakras. While the palms have openings to allow the movement of energy, they don't generate energy in the same manner as do chakras; rather, they are conduits for energy. Perhaps confusion regarding what is or is not a chakra originates from defining points of the *nadi* schematic as being chakras.

Nadis

Nadis—energy pathways throughout the body—were detailed thousands of years ago as part of traditional Indian medicine. Nadis transport *prana*, the energy equivalent of qi. These channels emanate from the chakras and gradually become thinner the further they extend outward.[10] This configuration is similar to the nervous system in that the chakras correlate to the

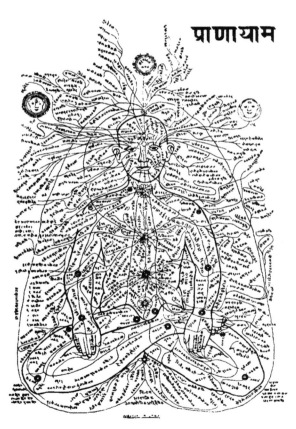

Figure 2.4. Nadis

An ancient depiction of the nadi energy pathways.

(Illustration courtesy of Wikimedia Commons)

central nervous system and the nadi pathways correspond to the peripheral nervous system. Although comparable to meridians, nadi pathways are more numerous than meridians and there are also thought to be some 72,000 points of stimulation along these routes compared with the 361 acupuncture points listed by WHO. On the other hand, there are three primary nadis channels whereas there are fourteen principal meridians.

THE ENERGY BODY

It is accepted by many quantum physicists that physical particles are an effect of wave structures, and that the particles and objects of the physical universe arise from nonphysical energy. Indeed, atoms themselves are waveforms, not particles.[11] If the universe is inherently an energetic wave structure then perhaps the physical body—of an individual and of the species—is the particle emanating from the waveform.

If so, this gives credence to a view of the world in which: a) the physical body results from, or is an effect of, the energy body, b) states of health are the effect of conditions within the energy body that then find expression through the physical body, and c) the energy body is an objective, measurable form, not just the effect of physical-based emissions of energy.

As mentioned in chapter one, Toltec theory offers a comprehensive view of the basic structure of the energy body, including uniformity, cohesion, focal point, and core. Here we will take a closer look at the energy body and the energetic fields relating to it.

Emanations
According to Toltec theory, there are specific vibrations or energy lines known as emanations, which are generated by a cosmological source energy.[12] Each aspect of creation has its own emanation. Thus there is an emanation for humans, for extraterrestrials, for plants, and for trees, just to name a few. Emanations pertain to all energies emitted from a source, be they a single vibration or a bandwidth comprised of various frequencies. They are the natural essence of a person, place, or thing.

From a cosmological perspective, dark energy also represents emanations from a source. A recent discovery, dark energy is thought to comprise almost three-fourths of our universe and to have a direct influence on our world and us. This revelation may require a new theory of physics.[13]

Stretching through infinity, emanations contain the realization of potential. While some may directly affect the energy body, others, which exist beyond the domain of human awareness, have indirect influence; still others may have no effect whatsoever as they don't connect, directly or indirectly, with the human domain.

Auric Field

Just as there are cosmological emanations that produce life, humans emit vibrations that produce what are often referred to as *auras*. This is the energy extending outward from the entire energy body. Oschman has postulated that it is a field of ionic vapor surrounding the physical body.[14] An apt analogy is that of an incandescent lightbulb. The filament represents the physical body and the glass represents the outer edge of the nonphysical energy field. Through the interplay of an energized physical body interacting with the nonphysical energies, the bulb emits energy: the aura.

Some healers, such as Barbara Brennan, have interesting schematics, which correlate states of health with the colors and clarity of the auric field.[15] It is important to keep in mind that the aura is not the energy body itself. It is the light emanating from the entire being.

Cohesion

While cohesion is the overall pattern of energy within the energy body, coherence relates to the interaction among all the influences that form cohesion. Looking solely at the chakras, it's easy to see that it is quite a balancing act to choreograph many separate forms of energy so that they act cooperatively. When we add the pushes and pulls found in daily life, the task becomes seemingly immense. Coherence reflects the end result of this orchestration.

Cohesion results from all influences within and without, so any energy assessment needs to take into consideration all factors, such as the combined energies of the chakras, the meridians, and the biological electric circuitry. A greater understanding of all influences and how they interact might well be the focus of future scientific research.

A key to understanding this anatomy is to recognize that your cohesion determines exactly what you think, feel, or otherwise experience. It is the first cause or underlying factor of all perception. At the same time, cohesion forms from our experiences. New experience generates new cohesions; new cohesions provide new experience. Meridians and chakras also play a role as they reflect and influence your state of health and so affect how cohesion forms.

Cohesion generates meaning. It drives behavior. Your job reflects a particular cohesion, as do your family, hobbies, religious life, and every other aspect of your life, whether dysfunctional or positive. When they are in harmony, so is coherence—and vice versa. Learn to manage coherence and you will learn to shift your cohesion. As a result, your experience will shift. Shift it enough and you may enter a completely new world. The many forms cohesion takes are ultimately governed by the shape of the container, known as uniformity.

Uniformity

Uniformity pertains to the overall shape of the energy body. There is a line of thought that the energy body was once narrow and elliptical and is evolving to a pure sphere. Within infinity, our energy bodies exist within a certain bandwidth, as do the energy forms of other species.[16] Uniformity is the attribute that provides basic definition to the organism, just as the defined regions or specific bandwidths of the AM and FM radio frequencies each have their own nature: FM tends to have higher vibrations and clearer reception but generally does not travel the distance that AM frequencies do. The use of one or the other depends on your goal. Uniformity is the overarching condition that influences perceptions and behaviors. It molds that which is within it and therefore defines what is possible.

Core Awareness

Core is the essential aspect of how an individual has been created. It is also a direct connection with infinity. Considerations of what is internal and external cease to have ordinary meaning as your inner-outer references melt away, leaving you with direct experience of your life rather than thoughts about it. The further you stretch awareness, the more you are able to touch your core. From another perspective, core and a completely awakened energy body are synonymous.

Focal Point

Cohesion can be measured or identified by the location of the focal point. In the same manner that an EEG map of brain waves indicates a state of consciousness, the focal point's position indicates the type of overall cohesion. Don Juan, a Toltec shaman and the principal figure in Castaneda's books, refers to this soft, glowing energy within the energy body as the *assemblage point*.[17] Awareness occurs, says don Juan, through the pressure of universal emanations of energy impinging on the energy body. This pressure produces an alignment of energy lines inside the energy body with those outside of it. This alignment then energizes a specific spot on or within the energy body. This spot is the focal point (or assemblage point), where cohesion becomes organized and perception is then focused or assembled.

Change cohesion and you change the location of the focal point. Sleep produces a natural shift in cohesion from the right side to the left, from the physical into the nonphysical regions. When this occurs, you can *see* a corresponding shift of the focal point. Common experiences

Focal Point   Focal Point Shift

Figure 2.5. Focal Point Shift

with *seeing* include perceiving patterns of energy resembling heat rising from asphalt or more directly *seeing* the light of cohesion that, to me, appears like bundles of fiber optics.

Throughout the course of a day, the focal point tends to flop around, albeit in small measure. For many, it may constantly quiver in place. This results from not having a stable relationship with the world. Plus, when the focal point shifts, you may initially feel disoriented. This is simply due to having no points of reference for your new cohesion. Anxiety, for example, can result from a shift of cohesion to as yet unconscious awareness; the physical body translates this shifting energy as "anxiety."

As mentioned earlier, states of health or disease, which are inherently types of cohesion, are reflected by the position of the focal point. Medical scientist John Whale, author of *The Catalyst of Power,* is investigating the focal point as it relates to health and healing. He uses two forms of technology: one using crystals and intent, the other using a well-machined, modern medical device that filters light through gemstones. He bases his selection of a particular gemstone for a specific condition on ancient Ayurvedic healing practices. With these technologies, he has demonstrated rapid and remarkable healing. He accounts for the results of each method as a shift of the focal point to a state of health.[18]

First Energy Field

This is the known world, that which has been actualized. You may also think of it as that which is most familiar to you. In essence, the first field is the order that has been formed or actualized out of potential energy. Reason is the capacity for self-reflective order and thinking is the enhancement of this reflection. But reason and thinking only reflect a portion of the first energy field. The more you suspend reason, the more you become adept at using the entire first field, as you have not relegated yourself solely to the domain of human-made, self-reflective order.

Typically we behave within a very narrow margin of the energy body. Thus we have relatively few options of behavior. It is therefore

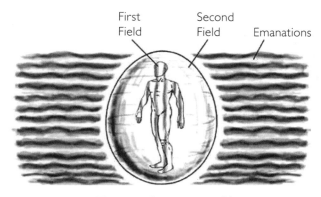

First
Field

Second
Field

Emanations

Figure 2.6. Energy Fields
First Field: Physical energies; order; the known world.
Second Field: Nonphysical energies; the unknown world.
Emanations: Some exist within and without the energy body; others reside
completely outside ordinary human awareness and are therefore unknowable.

considered unreasonable to be able to *see* auras, to heal with a simple
movement of energy, or to imagine entirely new worlds into existence.
The more you expand through your energy body, the more order you
have at your disposal and the more knowledge you have. One effect
is that what once was unimaginable becomes the order of the day.
Stepping out of reason's self-generated order you rest more easily within
a natural order. Procedures for stretching through the energy body, and
the means to manage this process are examined throughout this book.

Second Energy Field

The second field pertains to the unknown, to the potential that has yet
to be actualized. Simply due to our current evolution, this is usually the
more expansive area of the energy body. By expanding the first field, you
reduce the second field. The unknown becomes known. One perspective
is that the first field needs to be constantly extended into the second
field through learning. Another perspective is that the second field pulls
at, and thereby expands, the boundaries of the first field through imagination. In either case, you are realizing more of your innate potential.

Both the first and second fields contain qualities or properties of awareness, attention, and intent. Awareness relates to consciousness, attention to focus, and intent to directing energy. All pertain to the general management of your resources.

Third Energy Field

In relation to normal human awareness, this represents the unknowable, as it is beyond human anatomy. In the same way the second field is potential to the first field, the third field exists as potential to overall perception. The postulation of its existence stems from those who have developed their energy bodies in such a way as to temporarily step beyond ordinary human confines. Perhaps the third field is also the basis for theological and philosophical doctrines accounting for life after death. Aside from this brief mention, this topic is well beyond the theme of this work.

TYPES OF COHESION

Cohesion can take the form of conditional or natural energy fields: the energy of hardened form or unbounded potential. Conditional energy forms from the conditions humans place on themselves and the world. These hard and fast rules intertwine to develop cohesion. Reality then becomes a state of energy reflecting what we have conditioned ourselves to perceive, an inventory of what we have focused on. In fact, perception is usually restricted to what we believe we are entitled to perceive.

Any given reality generates conditional fields. Accordingly, reality by any measure is contrived. The underlying conditions of a reality establish the boundaries of what may be actualized; they form a blueprint for a complete sequence of events. Unless we actually participate with the conditions forming a reality, it remains in the realm of potential. Only by behaving in accordance with it, says don Juan, does it become realized.[19]

Typically, we have accepted the condition that the world is made up of material, concrete objects. And from there we build aircraft and automobiles to enable our energy bodies to travel. In a different version of reality, we might learn to travel by actualizing potentials of imagination. Indeed, learning to transport their bodies through time and space was one of the ancient Toltecs' great discoveries.[20] They were able to do so because they accepted an expanded energy reality and allowed that force to entrain their energy, and thereby their perception, along new lines.

Another type of cohesion, available to us all, is the natural energy field. For most of us, the majority of it rests in potential. This is energy that has no form and yet contains form. As we realize its potential we keep growing beyond the conditions that we encounter at each stage of growth. Evolving to a natural state means that we have grown beyond all conditional forms and energies particular to any reality. We can *be* without the context and guidance a worldview provides. Having a natural field means we are fully connected to, and are in harmony with, source energy: the quintessential natural field.

Achieving a natural field results from awakening the complete energy body. The further we extend the first field, the closer we are to achieving an actualized natural field. The activation of core is equivalent with having developed a natural field. As mentioned earlier, this is consistent with Maslow's concept of self-actualization and Jung's thoughts on individuation.

First Field   Second Field   Emanations

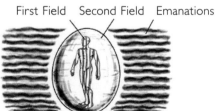 

Conditional Energy Field   Natural Energy Field

Figure 2.7.

The diagram on the left symbolizes how a conditional energy field blocks perception from the emanations, and, therefore, from a natural flow. A natural energy field supports harmony and balance with the world at large.

A conditional field may or may not resonate with a natural field. One conditional field may cause poor coherence within the energy body while another strengthens coherence. One value of the classic metaphysical systems is that they provide a conditional field that resonates with the natural field, thereby allowing an awakening and integration of natural field cohesion. By pointing the way to individuation, for instance, they employ a cosmology and method that provides a foundation to step outside the method. For this to fully occur, at some point we must therefore leave even such a helpful system behind. Otherwise, the conditional field remains in place rather than acting as a stepping-stone to a natural field.

CORNERSTONES OF PERCEPTION

Another of the unique offerings of Toltec philosophy is that of presenting a distinct organization of perceptual abilities, which I call *cornerstones of perception or awareness* and don Juan called the *eight points of the totality of being*. They are reason, talking, feeling, imagination, *seeing, will*, and the three energy fields. While don Juan taught the third

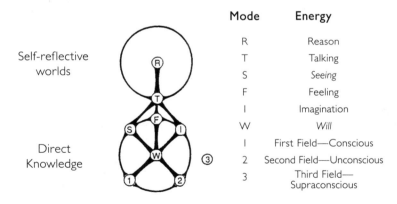

Figure 2.8. The Cornerstones of Perception
This diagram indicates the spheres of influence regarding the abilities of perception outlined by Toltecs. (This diagram is used with the kind permission of publisher and author, Norbert Classen, *Das Wissen der Tolteken*, Freiburg, Germany: Hans-Nietsch-Verlag, 2002.)

field, he did not use it to describe the "eight points." I included it in the cornerstones to highlight its importance in examining our range of perception. The cornerstones are scattered about the body, not in a straight line as are the chakras.[21] Yet all perceptions of the chakras may be accounted for by the cornerstones and vice versa. It is easy to work with both, as each is energy based. In this manner, they share a common origin. The value of knowing both languages is flexibility.

Each cornerstone has a specific location in the physical body. Reason and talking are in the brain, while imagination is found in the adrenal glands and *seeing* is relegated to the pancreas. It is interesting to note that both Eastern and Western metaphysical systems often associate dreaming (imagination) with the adrenal glands.

Cornerstone	Location	Perception
Reason	Brain	Organizes information from the intellect and five physical senses. Produces human-made order.
Talking	Brain	Indirect representation of the world. Translates information from the other senses.
Feeling	Heart	The affective aspect of sensing of self and environment and corresponding aspect of emotions.
Imagination	Liver	Dreamlike perceptions, both spurious and concrete.
Seeing	Pancreas	Direct, immediate awareness of energy.
Will	Abdomen	An integrated and focused cohesion activates this direct connection with the environment. Manages other cornerstones.
First Energy Field	Right side of the body	Realized, learned order of the known world.
Second Energy Field	Left side of the body	The potential of the unknown.
Third Energy Field	Outside human awareness	The unknowable. Energy that has no connection with ordinary human awareness.

To further elaborate:

Reason. Reason offers a means to make order out of the immensity of the world. It collapses infinity into a usable format. However, it is rooted in subject-object relationships and therefore provides indirect, or representational, awareness. Perceptions of something "out there" are measured in relation to oneself. The world then becomes objectified. While it is a marvelous tool, this cornerstone typically takes command of perception and inhibits awareness of being directly and intimately connected with the world.

The brain, the location of this cornerstone, is but one part of the body. Our body fully connects us with infinity, while reason is responsible for only that portion of infinity that has thus far been rendered reasonable. It offers a delectable slice of the pie but it is only a slice. When we have a more full-bodied relationship to ourselves, we awaken our innate, and often latent, capacities of perception.

Talking. Talking maintains order. We tend to take the order generated by reason and then constantly bounce that information around inside cohesion, like bouncing an image off a set of internal mirrors. The reflection becomes what is viewed as being accurate if not real. Talking and its correlate, thinking, therefore, may restrain awareness by keeping us in a self-reflective world. For all its majesty, talking, like reason, its source, becomes a force to harden cohesion; it removes awareness from infinity rather than offering steps to encounter it.

There is an order beyond talking and reason. It is the order of the natural cosmos, the order of pure potential. Interestingly, talking about potential makes infinity seem reasonable, and reflecting on the world from a variety of angles helps make it possible for us to drop thinking and reason to awaken other cornerstones. The more we discover the relativity of worldviews, the less sway they hold.

Feeling. This pertains to the affective part of us, both the seemingly passive perception of listening to the world in a different way and the active emotive abilities. Each influences the other and the terms "feeling" and "emotion" are often used interchangeably. Feeling is a principal navigational tool in a world of energy. It connects the physical and nonphysical worlds as well as those aspects within human anatomy. Oschman holds that there is a biomagnetic field associated with the heart that extends indefinitely into space.[22] This field connects us directly with the world and enables us to better sense, and make sense of, our environment. Recognizing the existence of such a field and then doing something about it adds weight to a view of consciousness that accounts for the value of developing this cornerstone.

The more perception is focused in reason, the less we are able to feel. Educating feeling provides wide-varying experiences that help expand worldviews. A casual review of history reveals that human-generated order changes, along with entire frameworks of reality. Feeling is a way to accelerate an ever-expanding sense of order. Indeed, through feeling we can tap the essence of a situation. We can also stretch ourselves beyond normal conditions and enter new worlds.

The relationship between talking or thought and feeling is important. Rather than remain in the reflective world of thinking, feeling lets us tap into the world directly. At the same time, it is interwoven with thinking. Our thoughts help govern how we feel and how we feel influences our thinking. One of the recent advances in understanding the human condition is the body of literature concerning the complexities of feeling, emotion, and thought. Led by Daniel Goleman's breakthrough book, *Emotional Intelligence,* there are now a number of books tackling various components of this complex realm, such as how emotions affect health, leadership, and the organization of reality.

In his book, Goleman points out the interrelationships between

thinking and feeling. He says that thinking plays a large role in determining our emotions and that our emotions are critical for effective
thinking. He also offers evidence that people often make terrible decisions because their emotional education is inadequate. Furthermore, he
relates both thinking and emotions to specific areas of the brain and
says that the brain holds two intelligences: rational and emotional. He
defines emotional intelligence as a set of skills, including control of
impulses, self-motivation, empathy, and self-awareness. When intellectual and emotional intelligence complement each other, both increase.[23]
Perhaps the area of the brain that deals with emotions directly relates
to the heart. If so, we have a correspondence of scientific and Toltec
models. This offers just a hint of the types of investigations that could
catapult awareness into a completely energized reality.

Moreover, in her provocative work, *Infinite Mind,* scientist Valerie
Hunt makes the case that emotions organize the "mind field," the
inherent capacity for deliberate human consciousness. In *The Feeling of
What Happens,* neuroscientist Antonio Damasio documents that emotion is a key aspect of reasoning. And in *Molecules of Emotion,* research
professor Candace B. Pert offers a biological model of how emotions
work and affect perception. Indeed, Pert asserts that there is no objective reality. To handle the immensity of existence, we must have a filtering system to assess what is important; emotions "decide what is worth
paying attention to." Emotional intelligence is therefore the meta-
program of rational intelligence.[24]

> *Imagination.* Imagination enables us to directly explore our energy
> body. As used here, it does not mean flights of fancy but rather
> refers to a sophisticated, disciplined mode of viewing and inter-
> acting with self and world. It may occur as a simple, fleeting
> image, a rigorous problem-solving technique, or even a full-
> bodied experience. In this manner, imagination is akin to enter-
> ing *heightened awareness,* a state characterized by increased inten-
> sity of experience, keenness of perception, and an accentuated

feeling of being alive. In Toltec literature, imagination is often referred to as *dreaming.*[25] Dreaming, in these terms, is a sophisticated activity with many levels corresponding to the learned use of imagination.

In this state, sufficient intensity makes it possible to produce a "body" that travels within imagination itself. At times, this faculty has been called *astral projection,* the *dreaming body,* or *out-of-body experience.* In such experiences, perception doesn't leave the physical body, as such. Rather a shift of cohesion occurs, and the degree of the shift may produce these different states of imagination.

Seeing. This native ability directly perceives the world of energy. It results from an alignment between the self and the emanations, or between internal and external energies. It also corresponds to awareness of or about something, thereby providing immediate knowledge and understanding of what is being observed. One might say it is accessing a different bandwidth of energy.

With *seeing,* it is normal that the daylight world becomes darker or a night environment lightens up. *Seeing* auras is often a prelude to *seeing* the full energy world. While the aura is a bona fide energy, it also just reflects a deeper level. When we fully *see* energy, the world may seem comprised of packages of energy. Humans may be represented as oblong, well-contained blobs of concentrated light. No physical objects are present. Everything appears as variations of light.

While Eastern metaphysical systems typically place *seeing,* or "third eye," capabilities in the pineal gland, the Western Toltec system associates it with the pancreas. The common denominator is that both pancreas and pineal gland are in the endocrine glandular system. It may be that using this mode of perception activates the entire endocrine system, which then permits us to *see.* Another common denominator is that the perceiver must develop a sense of oneness with the world for *seeing* to activate.

Yet another is that we must step out of thinking and reason to engage the world directly.

Will. The cornerstones of feeling, *seeing,* and imagination are all direct modes of perception centered at *will,* while reason and talking are indirect aspects centered in the brain. This separation of abilities is not a Toltec artifice; it has been expounded upon in classic Eastern and Western philosophies. In his book, *The World as Will and Representation,* for example, nineteenth century German philosopher Arthur Schopenhauer makes a case for direct and indirect faculties of perception.[26]

Will is also the raw energy existing throughout the universe. Maybe it is the *Star Wars* "Force." Through personal *will* this energy is at our disposal. The ability to change awareness, and so manage *will,* results from the application of intent. Through intent we shift and then restabilize our cohesion. We can intend to walk, for example, or to imagine. The basics of it are that we can intend and that intending produces results.

Will is the dominant part of human energetic anatomy, the central energetic system. It commands all of the other cornerstones. In the Toltec model, the central nervous system (brain) is a minor epicenter and the *will* (gut) is a major epicenter of human perceptual anatomy. The "brain-gut axis," as it is called, is well-documented scientifically.[27] Of note is that there are chemical compounds, neurotransmitters, in the human intestines that help form a pathway of significant influence between the central nervous system and the enteric nervous system found in the gut. A reaction in the intestines (due to a milk allergy, for instance) could affect the brain and so influence behavior. The Toltec model could be a more advanced rendering of how the gut affects overall perception.

Will as used here is an energy, not a concept. It is not dedication, commitment, or persistence. It's a force. It's the binding vortex of the cornerstones. As energy, it directly and immediately connects us with the whole fluid world of energy. Indeed, managing our cohesion and our cornerstones—achieving alignments of energy—is performed with *will*.

On a universal level, *will* is the substance of vibrations of energy, natural emanations that affect us in many ways. Hence we sense heat and cold. In the more rarified forms of energy, we can feel it and *see* it. In its various material forms, we can touch and smell it, taste and hear it. If it is dense enough, we can sit on it. Or we can mold it and fly through the air in it as we do with airplanes. More universally, emanations are the stuff of the universe, forming creatures upon creatures and worlds upon worlds. Personal *will,* then, is our meeting point with the universe.

The three energy fields. The three energy fields are the final three cornerstones of perception. Their operation can be better understood by considering them in the light of the compelling psychological construct developed by Carl Jung.

THE PSYCHOLOGY OF AN ENERGETIC ANATOMY

Jung helped to illuminate the nature of the psyche, which he thought of as our complete mind and all knowledge rooted in it. However, he did not equate it with the conscious part of awareness, as he recognized that it in large measure functions unconsciously.[28]

He also thought that, while mind and body influence one another, they have separate dynamics, not unlike the distinction between the physical and energy bodies. Jung also put forward a model of what mind is and how it works, a schematic comprised of consciousness, unconsciousness, and the personal and collective attributes of each. Models, according to Jung, are a means of exploring fields of inquiry. They do not make something so; they allow the observation of useful constructs.[29]

The Conscious: First Energy Field

Jung articulated his view that humans have a type of consciousness where the unconscious predominates, and also have a consciousness where self-consciousness predominates.[30] The first energy field represents the conscious aspect of our overall awareness. Its cultivation enables a greater sense of the natural order and so provides the stepping-stone away from reason. The first field, in turn, reflects that portion of consciousness ruled by self-consciousness or that which has become known to the individual. Typically only a slice of the first field has been awakened. This dynamic is mirrored physiologically, in that only a small portion of the brain is used.

The Unconscious: Second Energy Field

The unconscious, from this perspective, is the unknown or the second energy field. The unconscious has a significant influence, but in ways a person cannot account for, just as we often have reduced awareness of the second energy field. When boiled down, Jung's concept of the unconscious is everything that is available to perception but not known. It is also that which is capable of being made conscious or known. Furthermore, he addressed the unconscious as containing potential; an order reflecting a real, metaphysical reality.[31] From this viewpoint, potential may also be considered to be an existing order, which has not yet been learned and so not yet made conscious.

Jung also held that the unconscious was a "different medium" than the conscious. Furthermore, the unconscious contains the personal and collective unconscious, with both pertaining to an individual's psychic connection with others.[32] Perhaps cohesion and uniformity relate to both the personal and collective unconscious domains. Uniformity literally forms the collective into realization. Cohesion may either cause, or be caused by, the collective.

The Supraconscious: Third Energy Field

The supraconscious, the third field, contains the conscious and unconscious, the first and second fields, and yet is vast beyond human measure. It is the unknowable, that which is beyond the veil of ordinary human consciousness. However, there evidently are procedures for placing the focal point in the supraconscious. In the works of Castaneda, this ability is mentioned as a hallmark of a new cycle of Toltecs who rejoice in the pursuit of pure freedom. They aspire to awaken the entire energy body so that consciousness can be fully placed into the supraconscious. One highly esoteric application is being able to burn with "the fire from within." This involves completely entering the supraconscious and leaving this earthly existence behind, perhaps even taking the physical body in tow.[33]

If true, this possibility adds credence to an energy-body model where the physical body is predominantly influenced by the energy body. A shift in awareness—such as the fire within that produces a resurrection, if you will—highlights such control over the physical body, indeed, the physical world, and carries with it knowledge pertaining to virtually any sphere of human activity.

As an educational tool, just the concept of the third field stimulates continued reexamination of the human condition. It also becomes the basis of a learning posture, an orientation to remain open and honest, as well as humble, simply because most of it is beyond the human capacity of knowing.

3

Constructing Reality

As we have seen, bioenergetics deals with the flow of energy within an organism and between the organism and its environment. This interplay of energies inside and outside the human organism is the basis for our study of how the perception of reality is created and maintained. The inside pertains to all that is within the energy body, such as cohesion and the focal point, and the outside deals with everything else, including other people, groups, and resulting perceptions of reality. The meeting point is uniformity, the boundary of the energy body. This framework provides a basis for a deeper understanding of how a tiny spark of energy deals with the surrounding immensity of the cosmos.

The two fundamental processes within the energy body—learning and imagination—correspond to the first two energy fields. Learning relates to that which has been actualized or realized, to what is known. As such it is in the province of the first energy field, no matter how large or small the cohesion, no matter the subject. In general terms, imagination relates to the second energy field. It is expanding awareness, stepping beyond what is known into what can become known. As such, it is a dance with potential.

Expanding and integrating the first and second fields—learning and imagination—has the effect of bringing more of our energy body to life. The third field serves to highlight the vast expanse of what may be learned and imagined.

ENTRAINMENT

Learning and imagination are both impacted by *entrainment,* or *alignment* as it is sometimes called, which relates to the ability of energy to shift or create awareness. Put another way, entrainment describes the process of one type of energy influencing another, by their coming into *resonance* with one another. Just as the heat from burning wood in a fireplace influences the temperature of a room, all forms of energy influence the internal and external environments of the energy body. The entraining effect may be a condition or other energy. In physics, this applies to two oscillating bodies entering into phase with each other. In meteorology, it pertains to one wind stream capturing another.[1] Your arithmetic teacher entrained your thinking along the lines of addition, subtraction, and so on.

Our social world develops through an enormous number of entraining influences that end up becoming our "reality." Confining perception to a physical world of objects results from entraining to that model of reality. When natural abilities surface, such as *seeing* (perceiving the world of energy), we have typically been taught to disregard those perceptions because they do not fit the world we have been entrained to perceive.

The culture of your upbringing holds dramatic sway over your perception. If you consort with criminals, you stand an increased chance of entraining to their energy. If you associate with people who are principled, you are influenced to be so also. If you overly entrain to a worldview, you become a fundamentalist. If you entrain to source energy, you might step into a mystical experience.

Even though learning and imagination are both subject to the mechanics of entrainment, together they form a powerful way to manage it. Learning is the process of transforming potential into actualization, which, in a sleight of hand manner, also includes the use of imagination. In turn, imagination expands perception beyond the known limits of reality and helps to quicken learning. Imagination can therefore be applied to break the chains of conditional energy fields. Learning is required to integrate the resulting experiences. Without this integration there is no solid relationship among aspects of self, between conscious and unconscious, and between self and environment. Without learning, you may become lost in imagination. Without imagination, you may become lost in dogma. In leapfrog fashion, learning and imagination work together to stimulate, shift, and stabilize cohesion.

IMAGINATION

As used here, imagination is concrete. It is not flightiness or something to be easily dismissed as not pertaining to serious matters. Imagination is essential to solve problems, to entertain new relationships of every kind, and to provide the spark for personal growth. Its home base is the potential contained in the second energy field. That is, imagination permits you to access, interact with, and manage potential. This relates both to the conscious and unconscious aspects of your life. Through the imagination used in your daily, waking world the second field feeds into your first-field physical reality. As a result, what has been potential becomes actualized and what has been unconscious becomes conscious.

While *imagination* pertains to directly working with the second field, being *imaginative* relates to procedures of imagination, and *imaginings* are creations or actual inventions resulting from the use of imagination. Imaginings may pertain to first- or second-field activity. Buildings, automobiles, and scientific laboratories are first-field imaginings. Artists often speak of waking from a dream and penning or painting a masterpiece. Scientists may speak of the role played by imagination in their discoveries, as did Albert Einstein. The concepts that precede these manifested technologies and skills were imaginings residing solely within the second field. That is, they were all ideas floating in imagination until someone plucked them out and produced them by being imaginative, by being able to stabilize their focal point within the second field and then bring that awareness into harmony with the physical world. Imaginings were at one point potential until actualized.

Imagination is one of the most powerful tools of human consciousness. It directly connects us with the world about us, be it of the conscious or unconscious realms. It allows the perception of potential and, as such, produces the worlds to come. How much potential may become realized hinges on a number of factors. Here we will focus on the disciplined use of imagination, something that provides a fundamental reorientation to self, society, and life.

LEARNING

Characteristic of the order found in the first field, learning requires rules to gather and make efficient sense of perceptions. This is where logic and the use of reason come in; they have the ability to organize thought. Whether the application is for computer programs, scientific inquiry, or journalistic reporting, logic requires the formation of a consistent set of beliefs or valid arguments. Without consistency, we can't build on learning to create more learning.

Although the pursuit of logic may seem at times to be tedious, an understanding of the concept and operation of a logical fallacy—a mistake made in a line of reasoning that invalidates it—is invaluable. It is important to be watchful of the logic that is shaping an argument, for it ends up shaping you and your world. It is a fallacy of logic to say that you are correct based on the use of force, or that you are correct because you are an authority on a subject, or when you appeal to pity to sway another.[2] Jumping on the bandwagon of what has come before or what everyone else is up to commits yet another fallacy of logic; it uses an appeal to what is generally considered to be true as proof that something is actually true. Even the argument "the scientific community knows this to be true" is a fallacy of logic.

These examples are often deemed universal fallacies of logic because they apply to all forms of logic, even those used by different professions, which have their own internal systems that build on prior knowledge and further increase what is known. Different disciplines vary widely in their overall approach to what is being studied, the technical terms that render meaning, the inherent structure or logic, and the applications of knowledge. So measuring psychoanalysis against mechanistic physics isn't appropriate. Applying universal fallacies to test their integrity is, however.

Logic determines the strength and therefore the utility of cohesion. This is a key to understanding what occurs in learning, which represents the stabilization of a new cohesion. The coherence—harmony or dysfunction among the components of cohesion—is determined by logic. Awareness of the fallacies of logic guides us to avoid weak-kneed coherence by providing strength through objectivity. Through well-ordered logic we cultivate the strongest, most resilient cohesion. Knowledge of the procedures and effects of building cohesion forms the foundation for awakening the entire energy body. Without objectivity, on the other hand, we go hither and thither, spinning on a wheel that has no true reference to the natural human condition.

Objectivity is a tricky thing. Damasio makes the point that while the conscious mind is real, it must be investigated as a subjective experience.[3] According to don Juan, the individual focal point position determines a subjective experience and yet the world itself is objective (that is, different people experience the same result due to similar focal point locations). At the same time, it is the individual's cohesion that determines what is experienced. Don Juan goes on to emphasize the need for sobriety, for clear-headedness, of which objectivity is a part.[4] While there may be an objective universe, how each person relates to it is inherently unique. Two people may observe the exact same building, for instance, but their experience varies. Knowing that interpretation is subjective is a measure of objectivity.

The scientific model is an exquisite example of a procedure for learning, a method that instills at least the sense of objectivity. In its rarified form, nothing is arbitrarily dismissed or assumed to be true. This approach enables a highly detailed investigation and illumination of the unknown aspects of mind, body, and extended environment. The prevailing view of reality in our contemporary world has been markedly influenced by scientific inquiry.

Yet in practice, science often becomes scientism. When practitioners become unduly glued to their thoughts, that creates a mind-set that prevents discovery. Novel inquiry into new models of reality and new modes of perception is stultified. It is at this point that the revelations of science become something other than science. This takes a high toll on individuals and groups, such as when certain forms of medicine may be delayed in finding their way into the hands of those in need, or different views of the nature of time, space, and our relationship with a greater world are summarily dismissed.

By its very definition, the scientific method is based on rational logic. Reason, though, is like the channel markers leading to and from a port. It offers direction and context; it isn't the actual thing. But what if you were to use other forms of perception, such as those permitting direct access to that which is being studied? Might you then have more data to examine, to order, to use? And what if these skills had been honed over centuries to a professional level so that a new method of inquiry was established?

This is exactly what occurred during the growth of classic metaphysical systems such as Taoism and the Toltec Way. Because more avenues of perception were used, learning was accelerated. And so they were able to *see* and accurately map the energy body. As a result, they produced a worldview, which included principles of learning such as outlined here. As with any approach to learning, the new principles were based on their new worldview. Yet they did this in a way that they remained opened to further exploration and willing to let their view of things become obsolete; a hallmark of objectivity. This reflects the very purpose of recognizing fallacies of logic—to have some measure to better learn.

Speed of learning is an effect of the Toltec method, and logic is a part of the mix. Comparing the two approaches—scientific and Toltec—serves to illustrate the greater process of reality construction. Both views, whether we are talking about the behavior of planets or of energetic waveforms, are based on empirical observation. Toltec seers simply use different capacities for observation, which result in different data and a different body of learning.

ENHANCING AWARENESS

As important as learning and imagination are, the more the energy body wakes, the less meaning they have. Each is real, as real can be, and yet "real" is contrived. What is considered to be real hinges on a number of factors, including personal and cultural meaning, survival imperatives, and the current map of reality, to name a few, all of which are environmental factors that impact cohesion. As the conscious area of the energy body expands, a new dynamic unfolds. Learning and imagination are equal parts of an active awareness that brings us closer to *being*. In this light, imagination and learning are part of a practical *method* to enhance awareness.

Learning applies to integrating awareness within the first field, and imagination is a great way to proceed. Imagination, in turn, pertains to developing the second field. It is, by definition, expanding awareness and therefore accelerates learning. Expanding the first field solely by learning more of the same known world is slow and tedious. In relation to exploring a grander scope of an infinite environment, learning also takes a bit longer, as new references need to be related to what is already known. Deliberate use of imagination therefore adds a vibrant dimension to learning. When used with the other cornerstones, learning and imagination offer a chance to dramatically leap into previously inconceivable vistas.

Using imagination produces rapid focal point shifts characterized by new cohesions. In a nutshell, imagination supplies the force to move the focal point; learning holds the new cohesion in place. The inordinate instruction and time needed for reason-based learning can be offset by the cornerstones of *seeing*, feeling, and imagination. *Seeing* permits direct perception of the mechanics of the second field. Feeling provides the sense of the experience, a relationship for personal balance and direction. Imagination offers conscious exploration of unconscious domains.

The crux of becoming more conscious is to learn through imagination that we live in the midst of infinity, a point that awareness of the third energy field stimulates. Not recognizing this not only produces stagnant perceptions but could also be the harbinger of our species' demise, as we will no longer be able to adapt.

Imagine Learning

As typically understood, learning often involves developing a wider and more detailed picture based on that which is already conscious, or at least readily available, such as new information found in a library. Learning in this sense is more like hardening a veneer of awareness than actual learning.

To a significant extent, learning in any form requires imagination because learning necessitates opening further to something. Even if what you are learning is the ABCs, you must awaken to new possibilities that the alphabet exists and that it can be used for something. Moreover, nonrote problem solving is rooted in imagination. Novel solutions are inherently imaginative. Integrating the first and second fields is simultaneously the grounding of imagination and the opening of learning. Imagination permits going beneath the veneer of currently conscious assumptions into the unconscious to allow new propositions to be entertained, possibly to the point of their becoming concrete imaginings.

Once the value of imagination is acknowledged, then it can be developed. Learning solely through reason has become so overaccentuated that we have lost connection with imagination, even though it is one of the most reasonable and essential aspects of the human condition. Imagination is a vehicle to enhance virtually any form of learning.

Learning to Imagine

The utility of imagination hinges on how well the potential of the second field is explored and then integrated into the first field, in other words how much potential becomes actualized, how much of the unconscious becomes conscious, and how much is thereby learned. In this pursuit, we can generate works characteristic of genius or we can become lost. While the focus of this book is positive development, awareness of the unconscious-conscious interplay also sheds light on many cognitive disorders. The writings of mystics and psychotics, for instance, are often similar. Yet mystics are able to integrate their other-worldly perceptions into their daily life while psychotics are ensnared by them, because they are unable to discriminate between potential and actual.

Imagination is a way to shift our focal point. As it shifts, we become aware of the nature and effects of the focal point, which reveals not only the mechanics of the energy body but the relativity of reality. Since interpretations of reality are typically projections from the known world, imagination sets the stage for us to become more fluent with perception and less bound by *projection,* a topic covered in chapter five. *Seeing* accelerates the shift and restabilization of the focal point, as we directly perceive the root energetic causes and effects of our observations.

The use of imagination is often hindered by the intensity of daily life. This is often accompanied by tensions and worries, by the requirements of making money, of upholding your place in a physical universe, and by the gravity, as it were, of trying to hold on to your worldview. All of these tensions and forces bind perception to a simple veneer resembling being conscious. When this intensity diminishes, it's like a screen is removed, revealing a free-flowing, vibrant universe of energy.

It is not that your worldview is an illusion; it is as real as anything else and yet is one of many possible cohesions. The energy required to hold a singular focal point position in place may drain your resources to such an extent that you can't reach other options of reality.

Since our education typically does not include awareness of imagination as a principal feature in the formation of reality, it is all the more difficult to translate the unconscious into the conscious. We are usually taught to dismiss imagination or at least relegate it to a certain role. Fortunately, thinkers such as Einstein provide us other options, if only in the often quoted, "Imagination is more important than knowledge."[5] Imagination, then, is not making things up; it is finding out what actually exists beyond the current boundaries of accepted reality. It is a vehicle to become more conscious.

The learning of imagination is like learning any other skill. You need a context to understand its nature, a desire to stimulate it, and a sense of meaning that indicates why you should invest your time pursuing it.

LEVELS OF IMAGINATION

In the course of learning, imagination achieves different levels, which reflect the ability to manage more of your energy body. These are adapted from Toltec *dreaming gates*. Don Juan taught that there are seven gates and in *Toltec Dreaming* I have outlined these and others. In this light, dreaming and imagination are one and the same, different terms that both mean the stimulation and learning of the second energy field. I will present only the first four; the remaining levels are esoteric and account for a range of paranormal experiences beyond the scope of this work.[6]

These levels reflect incremental expansion of the first field through the energy body. Learning is often defined as a lasting change in behavior,[7] and this is exactly what the expansion of the first field produces. The path with heart is a prime example, which is dealt with later in the book. With each new level, more insights and abilities are gained. How these may be expressed in your daily world depends on you. However, because of the human species' uniformity, most everyone experiences common denominators in the levels of imagination.

Level One

This is the beginning of intentionally entering the second field. In waking life, imagination often makes itself known in an assortment of ways—intense imagery, flights of seeming fancy, and so on. Level one, however, is that of consciously entering the home ground of imagination.

In the beginning, imagination is akin to meditation. Meditative exercises often begin by sitting quietly and relaxed with eyes closed. To stimulate this level of imagination, you then pay attention to the emerging darkness as though you were falling asleep. Attend to the darkness until you find yourself immersed in a heavy, but not unpleasant, blackness. This is the precursor to properly tapping into imagination. It is also a way to simply recharge your energy; being in such a state for ten hours may seem like mere minutes. Being able to reside in the blackness is a significant step, so don't think you are not accomplishing anything just because "nothing is occurring."

The next step is to entertain whatever images emerge from the blackness. At first, you may not notice images. Gently gazing in the direction of your forehead with your eyes closed may help. Let the images come and go as they may. Practicing with purpose and patience will help you to turn the corners of perception. Eventually you will learn to stabilize and direct these images.

Level Two

Attaining the second level will allow you to behave from within imagination. It rests on having learned to maintain a stream of images, or to "control the dream," to put it another way. You may even find yourself entering the stream of images and flowing with them in a manner similar to waking life. This is characteristic of *lucid dreaming*, or becoming awake within a dream. [8]

In level two, you can also control your imagination by changing the terrain. Normally, dreams change: dream-to-dream, scene-to-scene. At this level you have choice; you have intentionality within the dream. To advance, it is essential not to get lost in the details or in obsessing about your magnificent achievement. Don Juan advises us to remain attentive to the experience without succumbing to it.[9]

When you are centered in imagination you gain a stillness that allows you to imagine from within imagination, to have a dream from within another dream. This is the way to prepare for level three: imagine a completely new environment from within imagination. From this vantage point, you are confronted with the multilevel nature of reality. It is also yours to simply enjoy.

Level Three

An interesting aspect of imagination, this level is akin to astral projection or what is commonly referred to in contemporary literature as out-of-body experiences (OBEs). This level involves using an imagination body—an imagining—to travel within imagination. This is a quintessential skill to solidify your imaginative gains. Specifics about, and exercises for, OBE are offered in *Toltec Dreaming*.

An OBE is just one form of *other-than-physical-body experience*. A key point is that such experiences occur within the energy body. While you may have the perception of being out of your physical body, such experiences do occur within the wider scope of human anatomy. There is also no "projecting" into another external dimension. However, there is a shift of cohesion, which enables you to focus on the interdimensionality within you.

A classic OBE has three components. First, consciousness is exteriorized away from the physical body. You may view your physical body from your bedroom ceiling or from across a room. Second, the localization of this nonphysical perspective has form of some kind. It might resemble your physical body in that you experience having arms, legs, shoulders, and so on. This is most often the case, probably due to the ingrained habit of how we perceive the world. It might also take some other form such as that of an animal. The longer you stay in this state or the more frequently you engage it, the form tends to shift to a sphere. If you choose, you can also replicate your physical senses. You can see, hear, smell, touch, and taste. Third, the form is animated and has emotions.

OBEs are not dry in the sense of just being aware, which may be the case in other types of psychic ability such as remote viewing.[10] As a distinct mode of perception, the out-of-body experience carries the capacity for different kinds of movement, feelings, and emotions. As a result, you can interact with your surroundings as you would from your physical body. The similarities to perceiving from within a body, plus the enhanced capabilities, make OBE a great way to learn.

From a bioenergetic perspective, OBEs suggest there is a shift of coherence that produces a cohesion that enables different perceptions. The first two levels of imagination involve shifting cohesion and creating new coherence. Level three requires you to stabilize coherence, which intensifies the experience. Level four is taking it all to a professional level.

Level Four

This is when you can target your OBEs to precise locations in your physical world, such as deliberately traveling to another city. For the purposes of this book, level four is important, as it reflects a marked ability to merge the first and second energy fields: an OBE is of the second field; when you can place your experience in your daily world, you are hooking together the two fields. At this point, a new mechanic based on synthesizing these fields unfolds. It therefore reflects a major step in awakening the entire energy body and places you firmly on the path toward actualization and *being*.

Advanced Levels

The three more advanced levels of imagination represent a step-by-step way to bend the energy body's uniformity away from cohesions of the human regions of the conscious and unconscious and into the domain of the supraconscious. In fact, this is the work of the new cycle of Toltec seers: a cosmological examination of the human condition coupled with exploration of the third field. Each level represents a shift and restabilization of the focal point, another marker that learning has occurred. At a certain point *will* activates, thereby permitting a further ability to manage the energy body.

In these arenas, imagination is vast and the experiences powerful and often tumultuous. The realm of imagination has always been so; but in these levels it is personally witnessed. Each new focal point position also changes the orientation to reality. It becomes possible to perceive regions of the energy body that were at one time literally beyond imagination.

Humans have a natural drive toward completion. The levels of imagination provide a means to take on the adventure of fully awakening your energy body. In so doing, your known-conscious world will collapse—or expand, depending on your view—time and again. Knowing the mechanics serves to buffer the turmoil and integrate the new. It is all a matter of learning.

HEIGHTENED CONSCIOUSNESS

There comes a time in learning when the energy body has been made so sufficiently conscious that it results in a heightened awareness. Colors are deeper, shapes clearer, and there is the recognizable emotional sense of being connected with the world. In addition, this state also enables the use of imagination in the midst of any activity, lending a dream-like quality to waking consciousness. As a result, some investigators refer to this state as *dreaming awake*.[11] This is appropriate, as in heightened consciousness the general landscape has a sense of viscosity that is characteristic of dreams.

This is not necessarily a *peak experience* where one may have a sense of a transcendent reality or at least that of an enhanced awareness of human potential.[12] Peak experiences are more transient, almost euphoric events, while heightened consciousness is more calm and lasting. They are related, though, as aspects of peak experience bridge heightened awareness and mystical experience, a transcendent state of consciousness, which will be covered in the next chapter.

Stepping purposefully into imagination is equivalent to entering heightened consciousness. It enables you to use imagination more skillfully as well as explore other modes of perception. *Seeing*, for instance, is not as difficult in imagination because the bindings of perception are automatically loosened, not unlike the Hubble Telescope being able to take clearer pictures of deep space because Earth's atmosphere doesn't cloud the view.

When the conscious domain has expanded significantly more than "mere" heightened awareness, you enter another level of growth. Then the terms such as learning, imagination, first and second energy fields, and all the explanations and details bringing them into focus become obsolete. In general terms, one of two things occurs. Either consciousness begins dealing with yet another model of reality, or you transcend reality as a model altogether. It is the latter that speaks more directly to

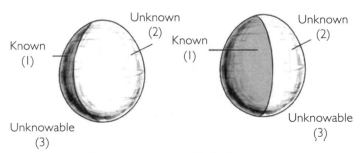

Figure 3.1. Energy Body Learning
Stimulated by imagination and anchored by learning, the conscious domain
expands throughout the energy body. At a certain level, waking awareness becomes
heightened due to the conscious interplay of the first and second fields.

being. You have reasoned your way out of reason and are in experience itself rather than experiencing a description of reality.

GROUP CONSENSUS

Imagine all of the elements that go into designing and building a bridge, let alone all of the pieces that go into creating an entire culture. Take all the interlocking concepts for the energy body model and then expand that to include each and every aspect of your life. Then imagine what happens when a group of people validate and thus magnify the validity and value of all these elements. The resulting consensual worldview ends up becoming a version of reality that is almost impossible to break free of or even see beyond.

Soap, hairspray, ships, automobiles, carpentry, education, medicine, the notion that the world is comprised of physical objects or of waveforms, God, and whatever else is part of individual or group consciousness are all parts of an inventory. The beauty of an inventory is that it provides meaning and relationship so you can engage the world. But inventories also constrict awareness by inhibiting the recognition that other inventories, other cohesions, and other worlds also exist. An inventory gives you things to look for, and if you see something that is not in your inventory you may not even recognize it.

Pieces of an inventory are established and connected through *selective cueing*, or deliberate focus on specific features of the world. Repetitive selective cueing is how inventories are built and maintained, to then become reality. An educational curriculum is governed by the inventory of the subject matter. An inventory can help you direct your attention toward a goal by letting you know what options you have, yet at the same time it can limit your options. Imagination, in turn, allows new bits, pieces, and chunks to enter consciousness. How these are arranged and used is a matter of learning.

Group consensus is not necessarily born of objectivity. It is an aspect of the collective consciousness; that is, it is an effect of shared consciousness and is subject to shared influence rather than actuality. There's great power when a group of people hold something to be true, but often the individual gives away their own autonomy to the group. At the same time, individuation not only requires finding and expressing a personal relationship with the world; it also hinges on finding meaning within the group, and being able to constructively contribute to it. Individuals are social organisms and so are parts of the group. Not taking stock of this alienates you from yourself as well as limits the capabilities of the group.

According to Carl Jung a person who does not break out of group consensus will never realize individuation. This makes sense: how can you find yourself if you only relate to the group? At the same time, he argues that individuation "aims at a living cooperation of all factors."[13] This is consistent with Maslow's concept of a hierarchy of needs, which indicates that social needs must be met first for a person to progress to the higher needs of learning, knowledge, and self-actualization.[14] (Please refer to chapter four for a fuller explanation of Maslow's hierarchy of needs.)

On the other hand, the binding power of groups—from peer pressure to ethics to worldviews—entrains perception along preestablished lines, thereby restricting inquiry from novel areas. This is the downside of social development. In terms of the energy body, the more you lock yourself into social considerations such as class standing, the less you will actualize your own awareness. There is great power in the collective and there is also immense power found in stretching into avenues not yet touched by it. You therefore need a balance of being simultaneously open and closed to all areas of life, while developing the art of knowing when to throw the switch in either direction.

This is the binary "open-close" requirement of learning. New awareness requires openness; consolidating the gains derived from awareness necessitates at least some degree of closing off. Both positions are necessary for growth, although the closed position of awareness is typically accentuated. While there is a natural drive toward forming the world into what is known, recognizable, and usable through enculturation, this tends to be overdone, causing us to step away from openness, to be less inclined to let go of one model to start fresh with another or simply to let more of the unconscious within self and society rise to a conscious level.

New social orders arise all the time. But if a new order is to be truly revolutionary, it must come from a deeper place within individuals who share a common bond. Otherwise, it is a rehash of what already is. People need to be moved beyond the force of their current collective reason and emotion by a greater force that offers enhancement of reason and emotion. Again, though, we have a blessing and curse, since a new movement can either liberate or ensnare perception.

Perhaps the guideline for whether a revolution can become a blessing is that of maintaining personal authority within a societal model that encourages personal flourishing. That is, the collective consciousness—the heart of the group—would hold that authority is found at the core of each and every person. This core value is synonymous with individuation and therefore serves to usher both the person and the group to higher states of actualization.

Understanding these types of influences and relationships fosters better understanding of the mechanics of the energy body. In general application, cohesion is formed through the effects of the inventory, selective cueing, learning, imagination, and all other entraining influences within and without. In the development of the energy body mental logic shifts to energetic considerations. In the interim, the world may turn topsy-turvy, so constant vigilance is required to remain open or closed at any given turn in your path to maintain balance and harmony with yourself and the world.

MODELS OF REALITY

If you were to take only one lesson from this book, this section is the one to bank on. Once you understand models, learning and imagination enter entirely new vistas. This is because your current reality, as well as all other realities past, present, and future, are models, approximations of the overarching potential of what exists. That potential has been reduced to "reality," to an extensive inventory. Inventories are *about* something; they are not necessarily what *is*. Models are simply a bag of options. They are a gestalt formed by culling interrelated elements of an inventory.

While interest in electricity and magnetism can be dated back to ancient Greece, for example, the nineteenth century marked a historical turning point in the field of bioenergetics. Many practical discoveries relating to different forms of energy and how they affect the human body were made. After Michael Faraday learned to harness magnetism to produce electrical current, Elias Smith patented an electromagnetic healing coil, Edwin Babbitt depicted energy fields surrounding the body and presented his work in the treatise *The Principles of Light and Color,* and Hahnemann developed homeopathy. Today we have magnetic resonance imaging, and SQUID magnetometers. Over the years homeopathic *provings* (a method to determine the efficacy of a remedy) have increased. All of the information in this book is a model; that of an extended bioenergetic view of human anatomy. Within this, acupuncture offers a model, as do chakras.

Within any discipline, models are often the benchmark in reference to which new ideas, procedures, and products are measured, tested, and examined. By making it possible to intellectually grasp a system, models enable further study of the characteristics of that system, such as a mathematical model of atmospheric conditions, or the mechanistic view of the universe. A viable model explains, predicts, and adds to the knowledge from which it was born. The use of the Newtonian perspective of a mechanistic world reveals why an apple falls to the ground, enables the building of magnificent bridges, and helps to accurately forecast what will happen when something is either exploded or imploded.

Models both evolve and fall to the side, because they are conditional fields and therefore invariably incomplete. The logic of a model consists of the arrangement of particular conditions. The practical effect is that a model always has limited applicability. For example, classical physics does little to make sense of teleportation. This form of travel—an area of investigation that is increasingly leaving the ranks of science fiction and entering science fact—is more in the province of quantum physics. But to build such a machine the knowledge of classical physics is required. Other models, such as viewing our Sun as revolving around Earth, become artifacts of an obsolete worldview.

At once resilient and fragile, models provide the means for exquisite investigations and create stumbling blocks to further research. These magnificently frail instruments are the joy and the bane of trying to grasp what the world really is all about. All coherent intellectual perceptions rest within models, structures that reason uses to reflect, interpret, expand, and consider. Each model reflects a singular cohesion, and therefore a focal point position. On a grander scale, the interlocking of several compatible models forms a megacohesion, if you will, and is the driving force of group consensus reality.

Models come in all sizes. A laboratory bench model might be used to explain and measure the effects of adding one chemical to another. There are paradigms: expansive, wide-reaching models. Then there are worldviews, entire cosmologies that become so ingrained that they lead us to forget that the "world" that is being "viewed" is in fact a conglomeration of interpretations. The difference between a laboratory model that accounts for a chemical reaction and a model illustrating a complete worldview is simply a matter of scale. As measured against infinity, regardless of the degree of scope and accountability, all models are but single, isolated pictures of significantly greater occurrences.

It is worth repeating that each type of model, however large or small, is a reduced version of something larger in scope. As such, it is a representation, reflection, symbol, or image, not reality itself. Any model functions as a principal determinant of what can be observed and the results of that observation. Without this awareness of the role played by models, any approach to understanding can quickly degenerate into dogmatic fundamentalism. As physician Gabriel Cousens points out in the introduction to Richard Gerber's book, *Vibrational Medicine,* "models are not necessarily real, but serve as conceptual tools to enhance a functional understanding."[15]

Models therefore need to be fluid and to change. While they allow us to make practical gains in our understanding of the universe, they need to change to allow us to have new relationships to an ever-evolving universe. Without such malleability, submarines, airplanes, and healing technologies would have remained solely on the pages of science fiction novels. When a more comprehensive model is developed, it is not that the new model is "right." It is that—in relation to the preceding model—it offers a new perspective, which is more abstract and thus contains more potential.

For example, the ability to specifically target cancer cells with minimal effect on healthy tissue, via new drugs and biotech advances, has produced a paradigm shift in oncology; physicians now approach the disease differently.[16] They have a new model, with matching technology, to specifically target diseased cells rather than place the entire body under assault with broadly toxic cancer-fighting drugs. So-called "smart bombs" distinguish between cancer cells and healthy cells and then enter the diseased cell and explode.

Some models, however, are not all that useful in the first place. Engineering professor Henry Petroski says that including considerations of failure in a model is an important part of achieving success.[17] In the world of drug discovery, federal law usually requires animal testing for many new drugs to help ensure safety and efficacy. Because of the difficulties of correspondence between species, the type of data derived from these animal studies may be of only marginal value or even inaccurate, thereby throwing a study completely off the mark. By contrast, certain other animal models have proven to have better predictive value about what will happen when a drug is given to humans; these are known as "validated animal models." The validated animal models provide a better basis for evaluation; the contrast between animal models demonstrates why possibilities of failure need to be part of a study. As a result, you have models within models within models. . . . This aptly reflects the complexity of constructing reality.

FROM MODEL TO REALITY: AN EXAMPLE

Reality formation is inherently a process of one model giving way to another. On a group level, inventories govern selective cueing as they determine the options of what can be called to our attention. The primary utility of models applies precisely to group consensus, which constructs and expresses reality. This may be on a small or large scale and may occur violently or peacefully.

The role played by models in learning and in the acceptance of new views is well illustrated by the history of the dampening and resurgence of homeopathy. A key to the efficacy of homeopathic remedies is the transfer of the essence of physical molecules into water; the energy pattern of the molecule is imprinted in the homeopathic solution through succussioning. When taken, a remedy acts on the vital force, the life energy, of a patient, which then produces a healing response. In other words, the remedy resonates with energy fields in the body, which then entrain the organism to a healing response.

Homeopathy was once accepted in the United States, but during the early 1900s, pressure from a group of physicians who did not accept such a model helped marginalize its use. Modern quantum theory, which can account for the imprinting of molecular energy patterns in solutions, is now beginning to explain homeopathy and other energy-based therapies of old.[18] With the emerging acceptance of energy-based models of alternative and complementary (CAM) therapies, homeopathy is regaining credence, as are such practices as acupuncture, laying-on-of-hands, and prayer. Perhaps originating from the explosion of books and periodicals offering CAM information, consumers have been putting pressure on physicians to provide more options for treatment.

Because of this grassroots movement, models rooted in various aspects of energy are blossoming. The energies of minerals, flowers, and aromas are applied to achieve particular effects. At the same time, some investigators in the scientific disciplines of medicine, physiology, and physics are tackling the role of energy in physiology across the board. As a result, the multidisciplinary field of bioenergetics is growing. By its very nature bioenergetics touches virtually every aspect of human endeavor; its healing dimension serves as a good illustration of this wide-reaching field. In part, these advances illustrate an individuated type of authority expressing itself constructively within a group.

This line of thinking is also present in the biophysical model, which holds that energetics provides a deeper level of understanding and description of the material world. If energy is in any way a determinant for physical actions and reactions, then new models, new variables for study, and new approaches to life will continue to sprout, eventually forming new ways of looking at the world in contrast to simple material, mechanistic perspectives. This is exactly what is taking form as evidenced by bioenergetic studies. As Oschman explains, "The medical and chemical-pharmacological models that have served us well in the past are not being replaced, but are being viewed within a more complete multi-dimensional perspective."[19]

MIT Professor Emeritus Thomas Kuhn writes in his book, *The Structure of Scientific Revolutions,* that a crisis is needed for practitioners to get out of their own way and allow new perspectives of inquiry to emerge.[20] The plagues of the nineteenth century provided such a catalyst. Kuhn also argues that a modern crisis has emerged from within humans due to the lack of answers that address modern problems. Perhaps the cost of health care and the debilitating side effects of many drugs may be providing an opening for new fields such as bioenergetics to take hold.

From the energy-body perspective, models help form cohesions. In turn, the ability to relate to any given model is determined by cohesion. If you haven't integrated a sufficient number of elements that form a given cohesion, you can't relate. There is no resonance, no connection, no awareness, and so no understanding. The reason that practices such as homeopathy, nonlocal healing, and other healing modalities have not been scientifically mapped is that there has not yet been a scientific model with which to develop hypotheses, theories, and then scientifically test these constructs—all of these being components of the wider model that makes science, science.

Once a model is developed that accounts for the mechanisms and effects of prayer on healing, for example, it may then be explained scientifically. Since healers often refer to the role played by energy, a bioenergetics model is a step toward a wider scientific recognition as well as toward an entire worldview, for which quantum physics provides the groundwork. Discoveries in the field are painting an entirely new picture of how the body works and how it heals. Many investigators regard their work as illuminating the very foundation of life where energetic occurrences, not material interactions, are the foundation of life. But alas, it is still a model.

Investigating the universe of energy will surely take us to new worlds and will certainly provide a high adventure of discovery. An understanding of models will accelerate this process and what may lie beyond. While the world of energy may account for far more than that which has preceded it, and may therefore usher us into a brighter day, waiting to be born are yet more new discoveries, new models, and new ways of participating with the world about us.

4

Expanding the
Boundaries

History reveals that reality changes as circumstance gives way to perception. From a flat earth to a geocentric universe to a quantum cosmos, our relationship with the world undergoes upheaval. And yet the changes tend not to be immediately cataclysmic or transformative. It took some time before the ideas of Copernicus took root, even after Galileo's validating efforts. Einstein thought aspects of a quantum universe just couldn't be right. Yet his legacy lives and breathes. And now adherents of the proposition that the world is fundamentally comprised of energy are helping turn the world upside down, or is it right side up?

STATES OF CONSCIOUSNESS

We can make this deliberate expansion of worldview function even better by understanding the process behind it. The work of psychologist Charles Tart, for example, helps to explain perceptual evolution. In his book, *States of Consciousness,* Tart puts forth the concepts of a *baseline state of consciousness* (b-SoC), *altered state of consciousness* (ASoC), and *discrete altered state of consciousness* (d-ASoC).[1]

In a nutshell, a b-SoC is your normal, waking consciousness, your normal cohesion. An ASoC is a state of consciousness that in some way differs from a b-SoC and differs sufficiently to produce awareness outside the scope of the norm; thus, an altered state. A d-ASoC is a stable altered state. When you've learned how to use an altered state it becomes a discrete state. It is something that is clearly and consciously separate from your baseline consciousness and may be returned to time and time again.

This can be related to Toltec theory, which elucidates the evolution of your energy body through different cohesions. Start with your stable cohesion that you use to get you through the workday, pay the mortgage, and raise a family: the cohesion and model—the baseline—of a "normal" life. To change the entire baseline state, you need to experience a number of different cohesions. This is accomplished by putting as many influences as you can into your energy field: art, literature, music, philosophy, religion, science, and economics. . . . How you relate to these, and the skills you develop, are between you and the world. That is the subjective element, the individual component of cohesion. The goal is to exercise consciousness in many different ways. This is where experience with learning and imagination pays off.

At the beginning stage of learning, a topic may be outside your daily reference. It may even be completely unrecognizable. An OBE, for instance, is something that is not typically included in the inventory of normal living. If you have an OBE, you may even work hard to forget it because you have no context for it. At this point, the OBE is an altered state. However, if you have repeated, spontaneous out-of-body experiences, at some point you will no longer be able to turn your back on them. Perhaps you will even start researching what they mean. You then continue your study and effort. Over time, you may learn to bring about an OBE whenever you wish. Then it becomes a discrete altered state; your efforts have helped shift, or entrain, your cohesion to express that ability. It is the same for learning any skill.

Perhaps you have concurrently been learning how to solve problems

Figure 4.1. States of Consciousness

Altered states directly influence your daily baseline state of consciousness. As such, they are essential in developing awareness. The above box represents a complete worldview, with the small boxes representing aspects of that view. When the elements of a baseline are rearranged, you experience an altered state. When this arrangement has meaning, it becomes a discrete altered state. When you command a sufficient number of "like-minded" discrete states, a complete loop is created and your entire baseline changes.

using imagination, as well as how to fly an airplane, speak a foreign language, and conjure up various science-fiction style cities for a novel in your imagination. If you develop these to a knowledgeable level, each realm of exploration represents a distinct cohesion. When they have all been integrated into a greater whole, your baseline consciousness changes. You are then literally participating in life from a new vantage point.

STAGES OF AWAKENING OR ONTOLOGICAL DEVELOPMENT

The dynamic of change from a baseline state of consciousness through an altered state to a new baseline consciousness applies to the *stages of awakening* or *stages of ontological development* of the energy body. At each level, you work with new concepts and behaviors. In turn, each new perspective and skill gained is an ASoC until you are able to produce that state whenever you wish, at which point it becomes a d-ASoC. When you have stabilized several related states, you experience a b-SoC shift. Each of these represents a cohesion, and so a focal point position. The main difference between them relates to degree or scope; put another way, the differences relate to how much of your energy body has been cultivated and actualized.

An ASoC is principally the random influence of the second energy field. A d-ASoC and a new b-SoC occur when you have integrated a new experience into the first field. The shift in your daily baseline state also means you have made a larger portion of the unconscious part of your energy body conscious. The stages of ontological development, then, pertain to bringing entire segments of your energy body into awareness and taking quantitative leaps of consciousness.

An ontological stage represents a major cohesion; it governs each and every feature of the reality you experience. As we have seen, our cohesion organizes our perceptions of the world and, in so doing, generates interpretations, values, ethics, habits, hopes, dreams, and states

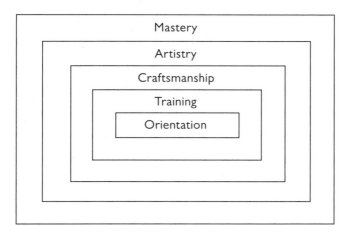

Figure 4.2. Stages of Awakening or Ontological Development
Each stage contains the others.

of health. With each change in cohesion, these change. Each level also reflects a domain of self-actualization, of *being*. A self-actualization journey requires being oriented to core for each step. Only the degree of proficiency in relation to core varies among levels. As you progress from orientation to training, and on to craftsmanship, artistry, and mastery, you are able to express more of your completeness.

One way to begin expanding the boundaries is to generate more experience, such as by attending an opera as well as a rock concert, playing a musical instrument, studying a different religion, taking a course in economics, playing a sport, and so on. By tackling things you are not so fond of as well as those you enjoy you will build connections and relationships within the energy body. Experience leads to learning and learning leads to knowledge, a condition where cohesion has been so well integrated that your relationship to the world—your ontological state of *being*—changes. As such, the developmental stages represent leaps in expanding the first field, the conscious domain of the energy body. Each level concerns stabilizing greater degrees of heightened consciousness as measured by the first and second fields merging. Practically, this means you are better able to *see* what you are up to and what effects your actions have. Ontological levels translate to how aware you are, and thus to how many behavioral options you have.

Each stage represents an immense amount of reorganization of perception, which is characteristic of new insights and abilities. Working with imagination is a way to directly stimulate and develop the energy body; learning integrates the experiences. The results are yours to discover. Otherwise, there wouldn't be any individuation to discuss. At the same time, humans share uniformity and therefore to some degree share cohesion, so each stage has common dynamics.

Orientation

If you are in the orientation stage, you have a highly conditional field. Cohesion is rigid and there is minimal fluency of perception. You wouldn't recognize an ASoC if it bonked you on the head. Your reality is pretty much fixed in place like a window-store mannequin. Orientation, though, means that you have stepped onto a path such as one of the transpersonal psychologies. As a result, you might begin to meditate, practice yoga postures, or work to enter imagination. It means taking the first step toward becoming open to learning about the world beyond ordinary constructs of reality. You now have some type of recognition that life is lacking and you are getting oriented to what other possibilities exist. Doing so carries the commitment to experience yourself as more conscious, more actualized. The essential aspect of this stage is an orientation to learning; your formal training is about to begin.

Training

This stage reflects the beginning of movement, the remedy to stagnation and rigidity. You begin to sense in a conscious way the intricacies of learning and growth. Whether you call it an apprenticeship or discipleship, this stage determines your relationship with your craft, be it Buddhist, Taoist, Toltec, or Christian. These and other systems all concern themselves with the development of awareness beyond the ordinary. While they may have different contexts, they often use similar methods such as meditation. It will be a conscious decision that you wish to embark on such a path, and whether or not you've a teacher you will need to find entry by virtue of your own wits.

As an apprentice, or disciple, you are fully engaged with your efforts to become more aware. Cohesion begins to be more malleable. During this adjustment you may feel like you lose touch with reality from time to time, which is actually the case. Another way of saying this is that you are learning about the relativity of reality, and until you can stabilize the means of reality construction you may feel lost. The training provided by your chosen system—theory, context, and how-to exercises—is designed to further orient and stabilize perception. In fact, your training offers the basics that not only lift you out of the orientation level but also provide the essential framework to advance to the other stages. In this manner, you will always be able to orient yourself, no matter the circumstance.

At first, though, "mysterious" events may randomly happen. You may have a spontaneous OBE or epiphany concerning a scientific discovery. As you grow, not only do you better understand how reality is an effect of cohesion, but you also begin to manage and use your experience at a more professional level. You can deliberately cultivate such experiences, transforming altered states into new baseline states.

Craftsmanship

At a certain point, you gain a professional relationship with your endeavors. You now step away from training and learn through application. You are a practitioner of the craft. You might therefore be a practicing shaman or scientist, for example. From an ontological view, this means you're now more adept at using the resources of your energy body. No matter the scope of your craft, the management of personal resources is a main feature of this stage. You can shift cohesion when desired and remain alert and balanced while doing so. You have firm understanding of conditional fields and what it takes to develop a natural field. You have also integrated the worldview and techniques of the system with the elements of your life. Formerly latent cornerstones of perception are awakening.

The dynamics of one stage don't become completely clear until you stabilize the next. As you traverse the stages, you will see that what once was effective no longer is. You always have to bring new skills to bear and behave in different ways to accomplish your goals. But this is what is involved in being a craftsperson of any profession. Discipline is the key to moving through the stages toward self-actualization, but it is important not to get lost in it. The labels and rituals associated with a given discipline are not the work; they are just convenient ways to approach the true issue at hand. The real work is in the *being* of it. A common shamanic exercise of orienting oneself to the four directions with the assistance of chants and feathers, for instance, may help you feel more emotionally centered. The higher skill, though, is being centered no matter where and when without any extraneous support. This is the knowledge—the *being*—learned from performing the exercise. Remaining oriented to becoming aware of core energy is the essential aspect for further growth.

Artistry

The successful result of craftsmanship is artistry, awakening the energy body to the level of having a natural energy field. A hallmark of the natural field is that learning and imagination are on an equal footing. The first and second energy fields have blended to such a degree that differentiating them is meaningless. This means you have become individuated, to use Jung's term. As a result, you are no longer bound to your craft. You can stretch your perception in any direction without the need for channel markers and supportive exercises.

While a metaphysical system offers a practical approach to comprehending and developing this scope of humanness, embedded within the training is the path to grow beyond the path. That is, training engenders a specialized conditional field, while craftsmanship represents a level of skill commensurate with achieving membership within a craft. Achieving the artisan stage means you've left the system behind. You no longer need that structure to grow. In artistry you are participating in a completely new manner with the world. You have become a conscious part of it, an integral part, rather than removed from it, actually living the time-honored adage, "in the world but not of it." You are completely yourself and completely of the environment at the same time.

This is also the domain of core, which contains all human intelligence. Conditional fields typically block access to this potential intelligence and interfere with the flow of information from it to a conscious level. The artisan is in touch with the core of their energy body, and life emanates from this vantage point. The more the energy body comes to life, the more you perceive the world from *will* rather than from reason. If you reach artistry via Toltec training, all of your cornerstones of perception will be developed. You will have moved away from the mental and more into feeling as a principal means to navigate life. You will be using more of your complete anatomy. For modern Toltecs, this stage is the guiding light of what "Toltec" means.

In general, whatever your craft, the potential you've labored to awaken is ready and available to be expressed in artistry. This is another way of saying that you are more integrated with infinity. What happens next is a result of your artistry as you perform intricate maneuvers with the cosmos. You have learned to live in imagination. By nature and definition, you won't know how this will be expressed until you're in the midst of doing so.

Mastery

Whereas the artisan has arrived at his or her core, the master behaves from that center. Don Juan has indicated that this stage of development is that of the *seer*, or one who has mastered the totality of being, which naturally includes the energy body. The prelude for this stage, he says, is that of the person of knowledge, or what I have referred to as the artisan.[2] From this perspective, the principles put forth during orientation and training are the basics for learning mastery. While *seeing* as a mode of perception is developed at each stage, a true seer completely engages a universe of energy as an integral, fully aware part of that universe.

ABRAHAM MASLOW'S HIERARCHY OF NEEDS

As another model of psychological development, Abraham Maslow's "Hierarchy of Needs" provides useful references. His schematic is usually presented in pyramid form to represent steps of personal growth. The more we are able to fulfill what Maslow labeled our "deficit" needs (shown in the bottom four steps of the diagram), the more likely we are to be able to fulfill what he termed our "growth" needs (shown in the top step). A person who has become self-actualized is able to suspend the innate drive to satiate the deficit needs. For example, such a person does not need social acceptance to complete a task. Conversely, a person may shun social acceptance due to psychopathology rather than for creative purposes.

The stages in this hierarchy are not mutually exclusive. A person can be reveling in creativity, yet when access to his or her studio is threatened, may drop levels and respond in terms of a basic need for security. The measure of the extent to which a person has stabilized self-actualization is found in the nature of the response. It is easy to observe that when someone lashes out at another it is because of feeling threatened in some way. A self-actualized person will recognize the threat to being safe but will tackle it as a solvable problem and so enter into negotiation rather than use violence.

Other key aspects of a self-actualized person are those of having a stronger character, being more open to experience, having a sense of autonomy, demonstrating increased objectivity, being able to love, and *recovering* creativity (which indicates it was at some point lost during maturation). Maslow also says that these healthy persons have a superior perception of reality, an appreciation of emotional reaction, and an increased acceptance of self and others.[3]

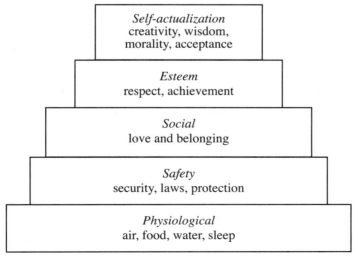

Figure 4.3. Maslow's Hierarchy of Needs

LEARNING PROJECTS

A developmental model such as Maslow's or the stages of awakening helps us to orient, assess, and direct behavior of all kinds. The stages of ontological development also have the inherent value of providing stepping-stones toward self-actualization. Each stage relates to how much potential you can access, which is in direct proportion to your degree of individuation. These stages therefore have both an intellectual and energetic logic. Talking about them facilitates entrainment as you are reinforcing these channel markers of understanding growth in your mental, emotional, and physical behaviors. You are deriving guidance from them, which is an effect of entrainment. Cohesion entrains perception to new cosmological emanations and vice versa. This is the basis of human perception, as participating with new emanations results in making the energy body more conscious.[4]

Learning projects are a way to dive into your energy body, to intellectually and energetically explore. A good learning project is to actively create an imagining in imagination, that is, to manufacture a specific situation or activity in your imagination or dreams that you may return to when you wish. For instance, you may enter imagination to explore the nature of perception, to write a book, to develop architectural blueprints, to use your heightened awareness to perceive the subtle energies of plants to gain knowledge of their healing properties, or anything modest or grand that will take you deeper into learning. The task requires learning how to return time and again to the subject you're studying. You therefore stimulate and stabilize imagination. And then in a traditional shamanic maneuver, you apply your knowledge in your daily, waking world.

Learning projects greatly facilitate learning how to manage your energetic resources. They apply pressure to shift cohesion out of its current state and change inertia toward achieving a goal. When a learning project is coupled with a purpose such as ontological development, it adds to the overall force. In other words, you are not using the task just to learn a particular subject; you are using it to grow as a complete person.

The worse case scenario is that learning projects keep you from becoming dull, lackadaisical, and resting within your current cohesion. In short, they offer robust stimulation of your energy body, which alone is worth the ride.

INDICATIONS OF GROWTH

Regardless of which stage of development a person is in, there are common traits that characterize growth. Only the degree of skill with these attributes separates one stage from another. Some of these qualities are as follows:

1. Emotional equanimity, reflecting increased emotional intelligence, more peace and balance both within and without your sense of self.
2. Fluency with logic, able to shift perception to at least entertain other viewpoints.
3. Holistic observation and participation with life, knowing yourself to be a part of life.
4. Enhanced sense of security.
5. Nondogmatic approach to life, able to live and let live.
6. Well-defined principles to guide your personal life.
7. Goal oriented.
8. Active in learning.
9. A sense of *becoming* with an appreciation of *being*.
10. Exhibiting deautomatization behaviors such as being more spontaneous and less worried.

    (Please refer to the appendix, "Energy Management Skills," for more information on the practice of deautomatization skills and behaviors.)

The stages reflect ever-increasing complexity of behavior, requiring the orchestration of different behaviors such as strategies, tactics, goals, and orientation. They also represent chunks of learning in both the first and second fields, and so indicate the awakening of entire sections of the energy body. As such, they pertain to how many emanations you align with and how well your internal energies resonate with them. The more cosmological emanations you touch, the more alive your energy body is; the more refined and harmonious the connection, the greater the awareness. Figure 3.1 illustrates this process.

At the same time, your sense of reasonableness may quicken. This, though, hinges on your ability to integrate new relationships. You need to relate to group consensus while not succumbing to it. This in turn corresponds to stretching first-field order further into your energy body. Learning and imagination must support, balance, and stimulate each other. Reflecting this process, your baseline state of consciousness undergoes radical reformation at each level and often within a level.

EXPANDING THE BASELINE OF CONSCIOUSNESS

The following sections pertain to experiences that move perception out of its cozy nest by stimulating imagination and learning, and thereby stimulating ontological growth. Depending on the nature of the experience or level of skill, they represent altered or discrete altered states. They also provide examples of various aspects of consciousness that, when integrated, help establish a new baseline state.

Psychic Experience

Psychic experience, or *psi* as academic and scientific literature refers to it, is typically segmented into two major categories: extrasensory perception (ESP) and psychokinesis (PK). ESP consists of those perceptions outside normal, physical senses. The basic elements of ESP are clairvoyance (*seeing* beyond the range of normal vision), telepathy (direct communication between minds), and precognition (the ability to know the future). We can add remote viewing as a distinct class. PK, in turn, deals with the direct influence of mind on matter. Examples of PK include OBEs, firewalking, imprinting images on photographic film, and spoon bending.[5]

Initial scientific inquiry into *psi* began in the 1870s, and the field received a boost from the spiritualist movement (mediumship) when psychical research organizations were founded in Britain and the United States during the 1880s.[6] Today, research has languished, with few institutions of higher learning providing courses, let alone research. Yet books on OBE, courses on firewalking, and psychic development classes can easily be found.

Empirical research points to a conclusion that at least some, if not all, *psi* is natural to humans and that it may not really be "extra" at all. Psychiatrists Gabbard and Twemlow have shown that prior to onset, 79 percent of those they studied or surveyed who had an OBE were simply emotionally calm and physically relaxed, that 89 percent wanted to have another, and that 86 percent said the experience provided a greater awareness of reality. Most OBEs weren't forced in any way; they occurred naturally and spontaneously.[7]

Moreover, it is now clear that U.S. governmental agencies have not only sponsored *psi* research but have trained people in its use. For example, a former military intelligence officer, Joseph McMoneagle, has revealed the inner workings of what was once a top secret spy program, the Stargate Project. Once a field operative, McMoneagle was later trained in a rigorous protocol of ESP, which is now known as remote viewing. After demonstrating great talent with the skill, McMoneagle was literally designated "Government Remote Viewer and Psychic 001," shades of James Bond. He was later decorated by the United States Army for his prowess as a psychic spy. McMoneagle now consults for corporations on projects such as finding the best geographic locations to drill for oil, as well as working with scientists in collaborations that have included contributing to the discovery of a new subatomic particle.[8]

The acceptance of *psi* hinges on the model of reality used; that is, does *psi* exist or is it scoffed at? But this pertains to acceptance, not legitimacy. A model that accounts for it can be found in both the Toltec theory of emanations, connectedness with the environment, focal point positions, and entrainment and in quantum physics theory, which elucidates energetic resonance, entanglement, and nonlocality.[9] Both theories hold that domains of energy connect with and influence other domains, that information from one energy field may be communicated or transferred to another, and that there is a dimension of reality that is not bound by time and space. From this viewpoint, learning the various elements of *psi* becomes just that, learning.

Mystical Experience

A mystical experience is one in which awareness expands to such an extent that humans are perceived and understood to be part of a greater, perhaps divine, reality. Representing a cosmological cohesion, it dismantles fences in favor of extensive and continual growth. It requires us to break barriers because it can't be contained. Personal accounts of mystical experience are often couched in religious terms, so this transcendent awakening usually finds a place in theological as well as psychological studies.[10]

A mystical experience awakens potential. It connects you with infinity as it stretches you further through your energy body and jettisons you out of your current condition field. It facilitates growth to a new stage of development. The term *mystical* should not be equated with the term *occult*. Occult typically concerns the experience, use, and application of psychic forces. An occult view may fence in seemingly supernatural events to make sense of them yet do so without requiring you to expand your vision.

Although mystical experiences usually occur spontaneously, such experiences can be facilitated by following a step-by-step logical path that leads to ever-widening awareness. All of the classic transpersonal psychologies contain their own staircase of logic. The Toltec steps outlined in this book serve as an example. At some point the logic is suddenly supplanted by an overwhelming gestalt of awareness. As pointed out by physicist Fritjof Capra in *The Tao of Physics,* however you arrive at a mystical experience, and regardless of whether you are a practitioner of mysticism or science, a common experience is that of having your reality shaken to the core.[11] Over time, what is at first an altered state forms into a discrete altered state. Rounding out the procedure, the integration of the experience leads to a fundamental change in your view of reality, thereby creating a new baseline state.

Researcher Valerie Hunt holds that "psychotherapists must envision this realm of consciousness as essential to an expanded, orderly relationship with self and the cosmic world." Noting that mystical experiences are often dismissed as emotional aberrations, she adds that they cultivate emotional intelligence and "are absolutely essential for comprehending life's profound meanings."[12]

Just as a certain pattern of stars indicates a particular constellation, a pattern of discrete perceptions indicates a mystical experience. If you were to have a mystical experience right now, you would notice several of at least ten distinct perceptions that combine to form this constellation.

1. A mystical experience is ineffable; words are not adequate to describe the experience. Although it is possible to recount the event to some degree, you clearly feel words portray only the surface.
2. There is a sense of surrender. You feel at ease recognizing creative forces molding your life. In addition, although you may have sought the experience, it came and went of its own accord.
3. As you touch the mystical, it enshrouds you in sacred wonderment. Knowledge beyond reason is yours and the authority behind the experience is self-validating. You need no consensus support to recognize its reality.
4. Typically, the experience is short-lived.

5. You are taken beyond ordinary time and space. While the experience is short, you may feel as though you have touched eternity. Gone, too, is the sense that you live exclusively in three dimensions. You now recognize a direct, inner connection with creation that does not rely on ordinary measurements.

6. You experience paradox, seeming opposites. You may feel as though you are in the midst of a fertile wasteland. The experience is rich beyond compare, yet there is nothing to hold. You tap direct knowledge that does not require thinking. You experience what you learn rather than apprehend it, once removed.

7. You do not study knowledge; you are knowledge.

8. You understand the mystical experience as positive and affirming.

9. You can integrate the experience. A persisting change in your personality prevents you from turning away from your new awareness. A mystical experience alters your life.

10. You feel fused with creation. You are no longer separate from your existence; the realization of oneness grants your life new meaning.

Some of these qualities are mentioned in the work of William James, often credited with being the father of American psychology.[13] Abraham Maslow also mentions some in terms of peak experience. He states that a peak experience carries its own intrinsic meaning, includes disorientation (an altered state) of time and space, and is always a positive experience.[14]

While this list gives a general outline of elements of a mystical experience, such an event is always unique, as though it were tailored to the individual. It is not necessary for all of these qualities to be a part of each mystical experience. Just as a cloud might prevent your seeing an entire stellar constellation, you might miss a few of them. In any case, the authority of personal experience supersedes any such guidelines. At the same time, knowing these elements is important, since you will become aware of each at some time in your growth through the stages of awakening. The mystical experience represents a symphony in which all ten elements blend.

A mystical experience not only opens and refines your perception but also clarifies your goal. If you were to feel the sacred unity of all creation, you would naturally behave more ethically. Rather than use OBEs for self-aggrandizement, they can be used to explore the furthest reaches of the universe or the innermost depths of yourself. If you can integrate the experience in positive ways, you seek to express your knowledge in positive ways, too. Through your experience, and the manner in which you express it, you begin to travel within infinity. As you do, your horizons grow, you touch expanded impressions of reality, and you realize deeper regions of your being.

Mysticism

It is possible to live in such a way that contributes to having mystical experiences. Traditionally, this has been the province of mysticism: philosophies, religions, and lifestyles that engender a mystical relation with the universe. These are high-end, classic metaphysical philosophies that provide a way to reveal the wholeness of life, including its divinity. A mystical experience is often a by-product of having such orientation.

Heretofore, mysticism typically placed the emphasis of religious experience on the immediate awareness of God.[15] The field of transpersonal psychology—which often includes mystical approaches—is revealing that a mystical experience need not be couched in religious terms. Still, through history, religion has kept this form of relationship alive with a higher order, no matter what it is called.

While the cognitive technologies of transpersonal psychology open us to possibilities and can hopefully lift us out of conditional fields, the interpretation of experience is governed by the entrainment influences of the system, religious or otherwise, which accounts for why a mystical experience often carries religious overtones. It becomes a self-validating experience, as interpretation ends up fencing in the expanded awareness. The positive side is that a conditional field is being used to pressure awareness into a natural field, into a direct alignment with a cosmic awareness. This is an example of craftsmanship that leads to artistry.

This is also an essential point in understanding human consciousness. Even when consciousness is turned toward the highest order of human awareness, such as in religion, philosophy, and psychology, it is still turned toward conditional fields. If they can usher you to a natural field, then they are the ones to entertain and follow. If they can't, and you still abide by them, you will remain relegated to the conditions of an arbitrary human arrangement of the world that does not represent the natural order of the entire universe.

The natural energy field, a complete conscious state of human awareness, exists beyond the confines of those systems that are designed to help you get there. Once there, you are always on your own—just as you have been all along. The difference is that you now have balance. Mysticism therefore supports the quest of expanding consciousness and a mystical experience transcends the model that helped engender it.

Greek-Armenian mystic G. I. Gurdjieff described essentially four main avenues of mysticism: conquering pain or commanding physical resources, faith and devotion, knowledge and consciousness, and a path that combines the others.[16] Yet in each branch, elements of the others are present. A person of devotion will realize more consciousness, for example, and vice versa. The various forms provide access to a greater reality for different personalities. Each avenue may express itself in elaborate practices or through very streamlined styles.

There are also cultural considerations. While the world's three major monotheistic religions—Judaism, Christianity, and Islam—share common ancestry, each has developed a unique form of mysticism. Even though they all engender a mystical relationship with the cosmos, they may not all consider paranormal experience or abilities to be viable for ontological development. A Zen Buddhist may shun the high adventures of OBEs, a Taoist may allow them, and a Toltec may cultivate them. It is also interesting to note that meditative experiences vary among practitioners. Electroencephalograph (EEG) research has shown that a Zen master might stay alert to the simple rhythm of a metronome while remaining deep in meditation while a skilled Yoga meditator's EEG doesn't register the physical-environment stimulation.[17] Different systems yield different results.

Buddhist monk and psychologist Jack Kornfield presents two principal schools of thought as *transcendent* and *immanent*.[18] A transcendent path strives for the higher order of altered states, such as mystical revelations, while an immanent path doesn't place such importance on altered states and teaches that everything needed is right here, right now, in ordinary time and space. Modern Toltecs are in the middle as they strive for a range of altered states to accelerate learning while recognizing that they haven't learned much if they can't apply their experiences in the here and now. As we have seen, the experience of altered states is needed for learning. By definition, you need to expand the bubble of perception, by entering an "altered" relation with the world, then integrating it to form a new baseline. This occurs with any learning. Immanent paths deemphasize the type of altered states that include psychic phenomena and mystical experiences.

Within the various forms of mysticism, some researchers hold that there are essentially two major divisions, reflecting outward or inward orientation to mystical phenomena. This division is also referred to as plenum and void, or *catophatic* and *apophatic*.[19] Plenum may be described as pure potential, all that is, or the complete fullness of energy and being. Void is often described in negative terms: "that which is not" as opposed to "that which is." Void is also considered to hold potential; beingness springs forth out of something else, which is beyond description.

Catophatic is of the plenum; it uses images to provide a human relationship, which allows the mystical to make sense through material or emotional representation. The apophatic approach, on the other hand, is held as an imageless, abstract portrayal of something beyond the normal human condition.[20] The important point is that these methods portray two viable models. But when dealing with the essence of mysticism, reality is always beyond the comprehension a model provides.

While it is worthwhile to distinguish the different aspects of mysticism, a significant point is that they are not exclusive. Certain teachings of one method overlap with those of other paths, despite their intrinsic differences. Understanding the whys and wherefores can help you latch on to the integrity of a school of thought to gain momentum. Doing so also helps you to avoid the trap of fundamentalism. All said and done, the various mystical systems share common denominators such as:

1. Recognizing a greater reality that is far more substantial than a material world.
2. Defining a mystical reality. Within this schematic, we find the clear division between occult and mystical experience.
3. Portraying a psychology or philosophy that determines an individual's soul (which may be the energetic, anatomical "core") to be similar to—if not identical with—the greater reality.
4. Offering a doctrine, system, or way to bring about the perception of the greater reality.
5. Providing means to actually align with, and so experience, that reality.

From an energy body perspective, a mystical experience is temporary freedom from conditional-field cohesion. It is enhanced recognition of the universe, which is characterized in an abstract, often spiritual context. This lends itself to the consideration that humans innately strive to become more conscious. A mystical experience can be understood in terms of the focal point shifting more to the core of the energy body, corresponding with an alignment to emanations that produce uplifting and cosmic types of awareness. The beauty of this interpretation is that since there are the objective references of human anatomy the causes and effects can be measured and then intentionally reproduced. In principle, this is similar to mapping out the cause of disease and then developing a technology to restore health.

Near-Death Experience

Yet another phenomenon that expands awareness is the near-death experience (NDE), which provides a firsthand experience with reality outside of normal daily living. I had my first NDE when I was eight years old. I had another while serving in Vietnam and a few more in a dream research laboratory.

The NDE that occurred when I was eight resulted from falling into a lake while fishing and nearly drowning. The lab adventures occurred at the Monroe Institute, which is located in the foothills of the Blue Ridge Mountains of Virginia. They use a technology that is known as Hemi-Sync™, short for "hemispheric synchronization," to promote NDEs. It was initially developed by Robert Monroe, a sound engineer and producer of several hundred radio-network programs. Monroe gained notoriety with his best-seller *Journeys Out of the Body*.[21]

The bioenergetic technology he developed uses sound to help balance the electrical activity of the right and left hemispheres of the brain. This automatically focuses attention, enabling the listener to more fully investigate aspects of consciousness. We could say that Hemi-Sync shifts a person's focal point, thereby shifting perception. Conversely, changing cohesion alters brain waves.

In recent years, scientific research has led to the popularization of a psychological model of brain functions, which allows us to clarify different modes of perception. In short, this model says that the right hemisphere of the brain perceives in a holistic, spatial, intuitive, and symbolically oriented manner. In contrast, the left hemisphere processes information in a linear, sequential, and analytical manner.[22] The brain hemispheres, which correlate and control the opposite sides of the physical body, may also be related to the first and second energy fields, to the right and left sides of the energy body, with the left hemisphere corresponding to the linear, right side of the energy body and the right hemisphere to the potential and imaginative capacities of the left-side, second field.

Hemi-Sync builds on the principle that the brain can follow, or entrain to, the normal brain-wave frequencies—delta (.5–3 Hz), theta (4–7 Hz), alpha (8–12 Hz), beta (14–30 Hz), and gamma (30–50 Hz)—outlined in chapter two. To establish this *frequency following response,* slightly different audio frequencies are sent to each hemisphere of the brain, preferably using stereo headphones for increased efficiency. If a 100 Hz tone is sent to one ear and an 110 Hz tone to the other, the brain mixes these signals and automatically produces the difference between the two signals. In this instance, the brain generates a 10 Hz *binaural beat.* The brain then resonates at 10 Hz, thus producing more alpha waves. As a result, the person becomes more relaxed and experiences more mental imagery—a state known to correlate with dominant alpha activity.[23]

To expand this, imagine establishing the binaural beats resulting from the combination of 4 Hz and 16 Hz. At 4 Hz the brain is resonating near delta, so the listener would gradually experience more perceptions characteristic of deep sleep. But a 16 Hz beta waveform is also being generated, leading the person to remain awake and alert, able to consciously perceive what occurs during sleep.

By entraining to the influence of this technology, I had clinically-induced mystical and near-death experiences as well as OBEs. In each instance, the laboratory experience corresponded to similar events outside of the laboratory. The NDEs occurred while entraining to a 1.5 Hz binaural beat, a frequency close to what is considered brain-wave dead. As I listened to the tones, I spontaneously found myself traveling in a tunnel with a vortex at the end vanishing in the distance. At the end of the tunnel was a gentle but brilliant white light. I sensed that the light consisted of a uniform field of energy of indescribable proportions. When I exited the tunnel, I *saw* a huge ball of white light. Although I sensed it in impersonal terms, I could understand why many people who have had an NDE thought of it as a tremendous light being or entity, perhaps God.

Approaching the light, I *saw* it as pure energy, or as a void, depending upon my orientation, which I could easily shift. When I entered the light, I felt it could be used for any purpose, that it is passive and value-neutral. I had the realization that perception there is not intellectual although it might be possible to take the intellect along for the ride. I felt the light was the permeating energy of all creation, including the intellect. I then went completely through the light and found that on the other side of it everything was reversed. There was a mirror image of the physical universe I knew in my daily life. My mind recoiled at the scope of this experience and the experience ended.

I think it is interesting that my experience corresponds with the findings of Raymond Moody, later verified by other scientists. Moody found a definitive constellation of experience that marked a classic NDE, including traveling through a tunnel, seeing a field of white light or a entity of light, and OBEs.[24]

In the lab a couple of months after my first experiences, we again used the 1.5 Hz binaural beat. Soon I kinesthetically felt a tunnel in my abdomen. I then *saw* the field of white light again. This time, I felt that it was only one bandwidth in the spectrum of existence, albeit the dominant band of the human condition. I intuited that the physical senses downplay, or even blind one to, other perceptions. I had a knowing that the tunnel was a representation of a force leading to the white light, to the core of something that transcends description.

This time, I dove directly into the light without hesitation. I discovered that we take ourselves far too seriously. I also touched what seemed like the deepest recesses of my being. The realization that throughout creation all realities occur simultaneously and in the current moment quietly exploded within me.

MULTIDIMENSIONAL REALITY

Mystical and near-death experiences plus the many varieties of *psi* reveal that the daily world isn't always what it seems to be. These perceptions are based in experience, not theoretical propositions concerning what the world is thought to be. To account for these experiences we must view reality as multidimensional, with more facets being revealed all the time. Their utility is governed by how they are spun into one model or another. From one angle, a report of *psi* is viewed as psychopathology, from another as advanced human potential. The bottom line of these experiences is that humans are capable of being more aware than what is typically taught.

Such perceptions can readily be accounted for in an energy schematic in which they are understood as shifts in cohesion. All such experiences cannot only be related to cohesion but also to other models such as chakras. That is, a psychic experience may activate the sixth chakra, while a mystical experience pertains to the seventh chakra. At the same time, the organization of all chakra energies is a principal determinant in forming cohesion.

Moreover, the integration of these types of experiences into a baseline state, and so into a version of reality, is not different from any other form of learning. The entraining influence sparking the experience could be the desire to induce what is read about in a book, a spontaneous resonance with an emanation, or by technological induction. The accuracy and objectivity of the experience hinge on how well cohesion entrains to the energy field being experienced and how well the observer has been trained in models and the nature of perception.

My lab experiences at the Monroe Institute revealed to me that we live in a universe where there may well be an infinite number of Earths, each representing minor to major variations in frequency from the others.[25] My epiphany as a lab subject has at least some grounding in science. According to science writer Marcus Chown, a "many worlds" theory is growing in popularity with physicists "increasingly accepting the idea that there are infinite realities stacked together like the pages of a never-ending book." Any reality, he maintains, could be very similar to another or vary in extreme difference.[26]

Another theory holds that only one material universe emerges from potential. All other universes remain only as probabilities. Yet another theory maintains that all possibilities are only that, and that it is only by the act of observing, by placing consciousness into motion, that a "reality" becomes evident.[27] Like any well-developed theory, each model provides at least a degree of utility to apply the science behind it, to make some headway in implementing practical outcomes. However, to gain the widest possible angle of vision of reality, the multiple universe theory is more expansive.

From an energetic perspective, a reality is a composite of frequencies, with each frequency producing an aspect of cohesion. An ASoC is not only a departure from the baseline cohesion but also accesses another frequency or set of frequencies. Because of its coherence, the many worlds theory signifies a d-ASoC. If new technologies are formed on that basis, it will mean a new baseline is emerging or has emerged, depending on the pervasiveness of the technologies. The end result would be that what was once alive only in the realm of the unconscious would be made conscious.

The progression of "reality" illustrates this movement of consciousness. Sailors once recoiled from traversing the oceans for fear of falling off a flat earth; Galileo put forth mathematical proof that Earth revolved around the Sun; a three-dimensional world gave way to a view incorporating time as a fourth dimension. Now, to unify all known phenomena, a fifth-dimension of hyperspace is giving way to "string theory" involving at least ten dimensions and perhaps as many as twenty-six.[28]

In his popular book, *Hyperspace,* physics professor Michio Kaku places ghosts and other paranormal experiences in the fourth dimension.[29] I would argue that OBEs are also fourth dimensional, as they command greater abilities in relation to our three-dimensional world. Kaku also reveals the dynamics of dimensionality by shedding light on why extradimensional activity is so mind-boggling to those living in the lower dimensions. A three-dimensional creature can't directly see the fourth dimension, due to its inherent limitations. It will perceive the fourth dimension in terms it can comprehend.

A quick review of your life will demonstrate that you live each day in many dimensions, in that you have many roles such as being a professional, a father or mother, a son or daughter, a friend, a musician, an artist, and so on. Plus, within your anatomy is the multidimensionality of the chakras. Added to this are the vertical and horizontal partitioning of the brain, other physical systems, meridians, nadis, energy body, and so on. If you then expand the "simple" three-dimensional model of reality to include ten or more dimensions, add a possible afterlife, other intelligent beings, other worlds, and so forth, it is not very difficult to imagine that we actually do live in a multidimensional reality. And there may well be an infinite number of realities.

5

Reflection and Projection

A key to understanding energy body anatomy and dynamics rests in learning how your interpretations of any experience develop. In essence, interpretation results from the interplay of inner reflections and the resulting outward projections of thoughts and feelings. In addition, as interpretation guides your steps through life, it is a principal interface between you and the world. It is therefore essential that you understand and manage the dynamics of reflection and projection to move your personal awareness toward the core of your energy body.

PROJECTION

Projection is the attribution of your traits and perceptions to another. Giving it a psychoanalytic flavor, projection is often accompanied by a denial that it is taking place, even to the point of dysfunction if not pathology.[1] From an energy body perspective, projection extends beyond simple attribution. The mechanics of projection can be seen as the effect of cohesion spinning and shaping all perceptions. Projection, then, occurs through the mere act of interpreting anything, since doing so results solely from the type of cohesion in place at the moment.

Charles Tart holds that interpretation results from a process—in which the intellect and emotions both play a role—of filtering raw awareness into defined perceptions. He maintains that we pick and choose perceptions and resulting interpretations based on preexisting beliefs and feelings.[2] Projected states, then, are a measure of reality. As German philosopher Martin Heidegger points out, projection determines what is possible in the first place.[3]

In this light, there are three basic types of projection: personal, group, or collective, and species. Personal projection naturally results from individual cohesion. For example, a person might say "He is angry with me," when, in fact, the opposite is true. A shared sense and interpretation of reality, or even a piece of reality, is group consensus. For example, a particular group might hold that Jesus is the sole Son of God, while another group regards him as being one in a long line of prophets. Species-related projection pertains to the effect of uniformity on determining what can be perceived; that is, the container plays an active role in forming inner cohesion. Perceiving the physical movements of heavenly bodies is one example of species-related projection. Ascribing meaning to this is an example of group projection—interpreting the movement from an astronomical or astrological framework, for instance. Taking the projection of our species to another level, experiencing the physical characteristics of having arms, legs, head, and so forth, is energy body projection as physical form governs capacities of perception and uniformity governs physical form. Change uniformity sufficiently and you have a new physical form (a new model of evolution) that gives rise to new perceptions and new interpretations of those perceptions. All three types influence each of the others. Depending on time, place, and circumstance, each delivers an entrainment effect to the others. Each contains the conscious and unconscious elements that shape perception. Each is therefore a reflection of cohesion.

Much of the work of the classic mystical traditions is geared to interfere with this normal projective process, to remove the stranglehold that beliefs and feelings have on interpretation, so that new perceptions can be entertained, making it possible to eventually arrive at new formulations of reality. The essential skill of suspending beliefs is known in modern psychology as *deautomatization,* interfering with the automatic responses that create all interpretations, be they individual, social, or of the species.[4]

The mechanics of projection-interpretation are forceful dynamics; from them, entire worlds are built. The dark side is that you lose the mystery of the world as you criticize others and even deny that those same features are alive and well within you. These dynamics are also at the heart of creativity. But to tap their creative potential, you need to learn how to manage the rigidity produced by conditional energy fields; otherwise your perceptions are predetermined by the prevailing view of reality. At best, learning will occur slowly.

Since being more deeply enmeshed in projection relates to a higher capacity for denial, we could say that humans as a species are still trying to figure out our orientation. In fact, as we destroy not only ourselves but our very home, the amount of denial could be considered pathological. There seems to be no prevailing awareness that a reality based on exploitation of material resources isn't working out. There is no compelling, wide-ranging consciousness that accepts that a new orientation to the world is necessary for survival, the most basic of needs. The need for the guidance provided by the stages is thus readily apparent. In bio-energetic fashion, the more aware an individual or group becomes the more they develop awareness of the environment.

SELF-REFLECTION AND THE CONTINUITY OF REALITY

The source as well as the result of projection is self-reflection. It is the glue that binds cohesion. The intellect interprets, defines, and arranges the world into a neat mental pattern, which is preserved by the stream of thought. The emotional aspect forms, reacts, and so arranges the world in its own way. This type of self-reflection is upheld by such considerations as feeling better than or worse than someone or something. In ordinary terms, both mental and emotional states reflect conditions that are present within a given cohesion.

The interplay between uniformity and cohesion produces self-reflection. It is as though the inside of the energy body were lined with thousands of small mirrors, each representing one inventory item on the shelves in your stockroom of reality. The mirrors reflect raw data into what we perceive physically, emotionally, and mentally. In short, how we interpret the world results from our thoughts and feelings bouncing back off the mirrors and influencing consciousness. From a wider angle, reality is the collective reflection produced by this stockroom of mirrors.

In psychological terms, thinking influences awareness and reinforces social reality.[5] Thoughts fixate the focal point, to use a Toltec reference.[6] If your focal point is at the position of "behavioral psychology," when you see people acting like they own the world, you might say to yourself that those people have been conditioned by their upbringing and by society to behave like that. If your focal point is at "Toltec theory," you might say that those people have too rigid a conditional energy field. If your focal point is at "mechanistic world," then the world is comprised of material objects. If your focal point is at "quantum physics," the world is viewed as being comprised of energy.

Every time you label something—an event, a person's behavior, a theory, anything—you are interpreting the world though reflection and projection. You are supplying energy to hold your cohesion in exactly the same pattern that gave rise to the interpretations in the first place. Collapsing infinity into a usable arrangement for *mental continuity* is the hallmark of reason. Although what is considered to be reasonable reflects but a mere piece of the vastness that surrounds you, it provides a measure of stability; at least you have a stockroom for reference. The magic of maintaining cohesion is that entire realities are built from sharing a similar focal point position with others.

Our internal dialogue aims and maintains perception and thereby provides continuity. Hence, being able to stop your thoughts is the best way to manage projection. A lull in your stream of thoughts permits a natural shift in cohesion, making it possible to have different perceptions and interpretations. Shift it a great deal and you will end up in a different reality. The same effect takes place at the level of the individual, the collective, or the species. By understanding the neatly woven wall of mirrors you begin to better understand cohesion, which helps you understand the force behind it all. Then you can begin deliberately transcending that force.

One remedy suggested by Zen teacher Shunryu Suzuki is to not believe in anything. This doesn't mean to believe in emptiness, but to suspend belief in arbitrary rules such as the transient forms of reality. Ninety-nine percent of thinking, he says, is self-centered. To step beyond this, he suggests believing in that which has no form or color, but that which is waiting to take form.[7] He is advocating a stronger relationship with potential, with a creative force, instead of being limited to that which has been created solely by human contrivance.

However, mental agility and stability are not sufficient. Our feelings also act as the binding glue of our perceptions of reality. Valerie Hunt refers to emotions as the "mind field organizer." As a result of integrating a multitude of experiences over time, a person ends up with a well-defined energetic signature.[8] This cohesion spins and forms perceptions along the lines of the interpretations that produced the signature. Reality has an *emotional continuity;* it is held together by emotional links, emotional commitments. How you regard the world is bound by how you feel the world is. This is why all heck breaks lose when you challenge the underpinnings of another's reality, such as in the arenas of politics and religion.

On top of all this consider *physical continuity,* or projection arising from the very physical world we inhabit. This is species-related projection. Our familiarity with trees, rocks, clouds, and all other physical-world elements exerts pressure to keep the focal point stable. Shifting cohesion into different worlds shatters this continuity. The degree to which any worldview expands relates to projection. A more expansive model requires more elements of projection. It is possible to end up just creating a more complex world without really getting anywhere. Growth through the ontological stages, however, is geared toward awakening your core; personal projection diminishes because you are paying more attention to potential, to ever-increasing abstract relationships.

AN ORIENTATION FOR LEARNING AND IMAGINATION

The stages of awakening—orientation, training, craftsmanship, artistry, and mastery—represent increasingly larger stockrooms, each containing more perspectives about life as well as greater capacities to *be*. Your inventory grows incrementally as you build a level and then quickly expands as you stabilize the next. Each stage is built from projection, a conditional field subject to those conditions (the inventory) that created the room. Each stage also acts as an echo chamber, providing both accurate and false readings about the nature of the room. The more self-reflection becomes self-centered, the more dysfunction you experience. The echoes then are phantoms rather than harmonics of reality; they don't have a solid point of origin. With shelves loaded with inventory, mirrors reflecting this and that, and echoes bouncing off the walls, it is easy to get lost. But that is what maps—such as the outline of these stages and of human anatomy—are for.

When you first enter a new stockroom, you may feel at a loss. The vastness of the new territory is too large to grasp and too big to feel. The first glimpses of the new room are altered states and may have no meaning to you whatsoever, other than signaling that you have experienced an altered state. As you become more comfortable inside the room, your expanded consciousness changes your relation to the mirrors and more meaning is developed. You have therefore elevated your awareness to having a discrete altered state. You learn in bits, then chunks. When you know your way about the room, you have developed a new baseline state of consciousness. You are literally living in a new world. It is then time to knock on the door of the next stockroom.

You don't need to throw rocks at the mirrors and shatter them to become free or to learn. You can just stop what you are doing, release the effects of the mirrors, and let new information and experience enter. This is the essence of deautomatization, seen in the capacity of rivers to clean themselves after they cease being polluted. You simply need to let go and allow your intrinsic, core awareness to come forth. You then can arrange the new perceptions and new conditions to adequately reflect and project in the new context, all the while knowing that at some point you will also need to let these go to reach yet another level of development. This dance of death and renewal, or release and regeneration, is at the heart of learning and imagination. It is the essence of the type of conditional field that can propel you through the stages to a natural field.

These levels each contain an energetic logic, with its own steps and degrees, just as in intellectual logic. You can't truly understand until you either have the experience or a sufficient amount of related experience to make the connections. And just like intellectual intelligence, energetic logic is subject to use and misuse. You may distort what is said based on your conditional field and likewise distort your relation to the world due to the same thing: an improperly aligned cohesion. Put another way, each stage contains its own nuances of projection. Consistency comes when you are focused on your core, as that energy resides beyond conditional fields.

Core Awareness

Core can be defined as the absence of personal projection, which is the quintessential, natural human condition. Traversing all the stages of awakening occurs as a result of aligning with your core energy. The activation of *will* is a by-product of this orientation, which brings the energy body fully to life. Correctly maneuvered, each stage brings you to a better sense of trusting your resources, decisions, and place in this world.

Self-reflection creates many conditions of imagination, some purposeful and some dysfunctional. If you are lost in despair or dwelling in psychological disorder, then your imagination will reflect this type of energy. On the other hand, if your mirrors are well integrated and polished for growth, then your imagination forms productive experiences. In each instance, projection influences the quality and content of perception. By definition, the degree of pathology associated with projection relates to the degree of denial that one projects.

Arrogance and fundamentalism come from perceiving oneself as "right" in absolute terms. On top of this, a person with expertise in one field may project that knowledge and speak with absolute authority on subjects outside his or her expertise. Being well-versed in the logic of one subject can actually blind one to the logic of another field of study. Core energy, by contrast, is more amenable to different views of the world; it connects with infinity and infinity holds all possibilities.

Maintaining core alignment is what enables you to sift through all the potential that doesn't pertain to personal and social development, as well as to maintain a balance between relative and absolute. If you entertain the relativity of the universe too much, you won't be able to sustain your own nature. If you focus on the absolute nature of the cosmos, fundamentalism will take over.

Only when you reach the artisan stage will you have navigated your way out of pathology. Until then, you will be in the throes of personal and group-related projection and denial. A quest to reach core is a way to stay balanced and focused. From this posture comes the behavior that allows you to express and fulfill your innermost condition. Attaining a natural energy field reflects psychological health.

In the path of learning, closure and core need to be reconciled. Closure results from and produces projection. As a natural part of learning, it supports our capacity to focus. However, closure also closes off perception and limits imagination. Core awareness, on the other hand, opens the gates of imagination, and the resulting experiences acceler-ate learning. As a fully awakened energy body and core awareness are synonymous, a completely conscious connection with the world results. Anything off center and away from core is projection, and projection results from having a conditional field of one kind or another. At the same time, core is closed in the sense that it is the way you, and you alone, were created.

The more you align with your core, the more objective discern-ment you have of yourself and the environment. This correlates with a movement of the focal point; the deeper you take your focal point into your energy body, the more you become aware of your environ-ment. This is the same dynamic of simultaneously being at core and extended throughout your energy body. As a result, you are aware that you are intimately connected with the environment and so are naturally more aware of the environment. Objectivity unfolds from this enhanced awareness. This is being-centered, not self-centered. The difference between the two makes all the difference in how you navigate life.

Another way of looking at this is to say that if you completely indi-viduate, if you reach core, if you have developed a natural energy field, then you eliminate the effects of projection. Individuation first occurs at the artisan stage and is refined at the mastery level. At these levels, behavior emanates from core; it is not tied to a group consensus of real-ity or to what is known by structured teachings, metaphysical or other-wise. The person is knowledge and awareness, not the representation of them. The person is *being*.

When you reach the artisan stage, you possess an inner calm and quiet, almost a sense that nothing at all is occurring while your world unfolds about you. Projection has ended and your connection with external emanations places you at infinity's doorstep. At the mastery stage, you have taken this awareness to a highly skillful level of manag-ing your innermost abilities, to the extent that you can step into those emanations, which are literally out of this world.

Timing

A principle feature of the stages is *timing,* the speed of your relationship with self, others, and the world. Timing is rhythm, harmony. It is characterized by your movements through time, space, and perhaps other dimensions. Good timing is difficult to pull off. Just think of having to orchestrate the pushes and pulls of several chakra energies to arrange them in such a manner that you may act in a consistent manner. And in our modern culture, how often do you find yourself going too fast?

Timing always reflects some type of resonance with core; it can indicate a natural *flow,* as in the case of a strong and direct resonance, or it can indicate discord. It is also an indicator of the type of energetic field you have, the locations of the focal point, and which stage of development you are in. Within the energy body, timing also reflects the degree of harmony between the first and second fields. It involves the opening and closing of awareness and the ebb and flow between learning and imagination. Projection, as it is not of core, reflects both poor timing as well as something that actively throws your timing off.

Appropriate timing is typically not something we are taught to be aware of, let alone to practice. To be aware of the importance of timing is itself remarkable. To be able to exhibit good timing at an ontological level is exceptional. Good timing requires the use of four-dimensional space, perceiving the whole of the environment, not just pieces of it. With self-awareness, you can better adjust to the demands of the clock; that is, you can navigate your job, relationships, hobbies, and other facets of your daily life that are governed by having to be somewhere at some time. Good timing by itself may not elevate your status in the world. It does, however, bring you more to life. A gesture given, a word spoken, or a laugh can all make or break any kind of interaction with others.

Timing is not fixed and rigid. You don't have to act the same way all the time. Timing is a measure of the alignment of internal and external emanations, and alignments produce perception. In the same manner, timing both reflects and governs heightened consciousness.

Thoughts determine habits and habits determine cohesion. The focal point becomes stable in a certain position when a sufficient number of interrelated pieces of logic have come together. The ability to move the focal point to a new location requires forming a new set of habits.[9] Timing is part of the puzzle of when to learn new habits.

Habituation occurs when you repeatedly experience something to the degree you become less sensitive to it.[10] The maintenance of habit thereby keeps you from feeling the original sensations. Your actions become automatic, rote. Timing falls by the wayside. You then become dull and lifeless, not even noticing what once held keen interest. Deautomatization helps prevent this calcification of perception; it helps you step outside of preconceived notions, rules, and behaviors. Using feeling, as a means to guide your steps, is an example of deautomatization, as is taking a different route to work everyday . . . as long as you don't make doing so into a larger routine than traveling the same roads day in and day out.

Deautomatization also offsets the effects of closure by refreshing, clearing, and opening up perception. Each person—if not each and every organism—is in some way unique; each has a core signature, reflecting innate timing. This is your unique relation to yourself and to myriad forms of the environment. Cultivating your core timing is an avenue of growth that can be used as a thread to navigate through levels of development.

You can use the stages of awakening to understand the relationship of ontological timing to core.[11] In the orientation stage, life is somewhat random. Often a person has no purpose, no sense with which to measure anything. During training, you gain a direction in life. The capacity to tap into an initially elusive concept of core starts as you begin to place your life in order.

By the time you develop into the craftsmanship arena, you have a fairly well-tempered energy body and have activated *will*. You can let go of preconceptions and entertain new possibilities; purposeful direction is well in hand. As you have removed tired and worn out behavior, life takes on a more novel flavor. Your life has been tuned so that you connect with life hour by hour. At the artistry stage, a natural field has taken over all aspects of your life. The journey has delivered you to the moment at hand, and traveling in the moment is the only way to sustain this level.

STAGES OF AWAKENING

Barriers of Perception

Corresponding with advances in learning and imagination, barriers to unfolding perception are also found in each stage. Termed "natural enemies," by don Juan,[12] they relate to rigidity, insightfulness, control, and aging. These barriers may be found in anyone's behavior at any time; they are not necessarily isolated to specific stages. For example, a person may still need to deal with the constrictive effects of a rigid cohesion after attaining craftsmanship. The artisan, in turn, must remain vigilant to the ins and outs of insight as projection to maintain a natural field. However, these barriers do characterize essential ingredients of ontological development, so assigning them to specific categories aids our understanding of their operation.

Orientation

If you are in orientation, you are trying to do just that: get oriented. This means that essentially you have no direction in life, certainly none in relation to your core. Your conditional field is therefore static and characterized by a lack of movement and suppleness, an excessive degree of closure, and the inability to form new avenues of perception. Perception is highly self-reflective and often without any awareness that it is projective. This general condition expresses itself as the feeling of fear. That is, when faced with a new prospect the inability of cohesion to shift may translate through the physical body as fear.

One remedy for a rigid conditional field is to gain a wide range of experience. Each type of experience represents its own cohesion, so the more you are able to develop a range of cohesions, the more fluid your energy body becomes. A guideline for this is to do exactly what you fear doing: in this way you face the rigidity head on. This doesn't mean being stupid, such as breaking laws. It does mean directly facing your life with courage. Over time, you will gain a sufficient amount of experience to be well oriented in life.

Training

At this point, you have picked the major ingredients of your life. You have a path. Now begins the training. This could take shape in the form of a college education, an apprenticeship, or other formal training. From an ontological perspective, it means you know what type of transpersonal psychology or metaphysical philosophy is most natural to you. You are developing a completely new set of habits.

All of this hard-won knowledge grants better insight, more clarity about yourself and the world. You are able to suspend projection to some degree. You more easily sense the potential of events, your imagination bustles with excitement, and all of this newfound insight makes you want to do new things. It turns out that that is the problem. It is too soon to apply your insight, as there is much more to be experienced and learned before you are really ready to do so. You need more depth to your cohesion; otherwise you are reflecting and projecting from a training cohesion, not a professional one. In turn, you may not act when you should.

Insightfulness is the first significant step to heightened consciousness. The fascination of this alone is enough to throw you off the mark. Maintaining such keen awareness requires an even better control and orientation to core to prevent you from thinking you know "the answer" even when you are only flirting with a new cohesion. A way to groom balance is to remain a bit cautious, actively wondering about the degree of depth of your insights, while still battling rigidity. After all, this stage is just another conditional field.

This is also the stage where you begin directly working with timing. To manage your insightfulness, you have to learn when to act and when not to. Without timidity, carefully feel things out. Align your decisions with your core values. Allow yourself to learn. The rhythm for all this is found in discovering when to proceed or remain still, to be open or closed. Within myriad potential, you are now learning a high wire balancing act of how, what, when, and where to engage your next steps. It is the initial application of your energy body. To become individuated, everyone needs to find his or her own way. The essential skill is taking concepts such as these and applying them, then discover what transpires, then apply what you've learned. A path such as this truly requires self-motivation.

Craftsmanship

Craftsmanship represents a high degree of learning and a sophisticated degree of managing the energy body, so that you can also control that which is around you. By the application of cohesion, you can determine the emanations you want to align with and thus determine circumstances. Now your energy acts as an external force to others.[13] On top of this, your now-stabilized heightened consciousness and insightfulness enable you to better perceive and assess what lies before you, enhancing your ability to shape your world or, rather, bend it out of shape.

According to don Juan, the ability to bend events to your desire makes this the most difficult of all stages.[14] It offers strong temptations that can lead you away from core into a overly personal relationship with life. This is self-importance, not self-actualization. While you may have acquired knowledge well beyond normal spheres of human activity, the cost is that of estranging you from the very quest that has thus far motivated you.

This ability of control opens the gate to the refined use of imagination, but it is important to remember that control relates to closure. Closure can easily turn into the abuse of power. This applies to all circumstances, large and small, where you hold sway over others. That kind of power is control, not freedom. It relates to marginalizing life, not participating with infinity. The guideline to transcend it is simple: never use it. True power is derived from taking part in creation, not trying to determine it. A key to success is to focus on developing cohesion to enter the next stage rather than to stop and admire your abilities.

Until you've reached artistry, every perception—*everything*—is an effect of projection. As you progress, you clean the mirrors on your stockroom wall. The trick is to keep polishing until they become translucent, until your light passes through them to connect with the emanations. You then *become* light, not a reflection of it. Although you already *are* light, remembering this is full of deception. You automatically, and with an ironclad guarantee, limit your connections with potential by your thoughts and feelings of how you fit into the world. This remains firmly in place until you become the artisan and have removed yourself from the confines of conditional fields.

Artistry and Mastery

Artistry is a relationship with knowledge and awareness, not with collective consciousness; the artisan is a force of nature rather than of the group. At this stage you have gained the freedom and ability to create your own inventories, to stock your own room. You have come to understand the wall of mirrors as reflection and have transcended their influence.

A natural field results from your alignment with your core: how you have been created, not how your personality has developed amidst social pressures. Individuation, according to Jung, is arriving at your "innermost and incomparable uniqueness." This necessitates granting precedence to self-realization rather than to the considerations and obligations of the collective. At the same time, Jung was quick to point out that doing so is not selfish but the fulfillment of one's nature. This requires "a living co-operation with all factors."[15]

The mastery stage occurs when you've mastered your energy body to such a degree that you step completely outside the stockroom. Everything that once was is now obsolete. Your experiences are yours alone. You may also step into the third energy field, thereby attaining a completely new sense of and enhanced objectivity about the human condition.[16] Whatever your goals or circumstances in life, you can orient yourself to mastery anytime, anywhere. The stepping-stones then reveal themselves.

Understanding the concept of the energy body occurs in the orientation stage. From there, you traverse the stages step by step, with the full use of your resources being the hallmark of the mastery level. Your insightfulness is refined and your drive for power is in check. You are able to maintain *being* and have a keen sense of *flow* in all areas of your life. Your energy body is so fluent you can gently enter and leave any circumstance by shifting cohesion to match those events.

To do this typically takes many years, so many that most of those who reach mastery are old and their resources are waning. Even though they have mastered their energy body, the barrier of age is insurmountable; they will die due to old age, if by nothing else.

Don Juan holds that if one who has traveled a Toltec path gives in to the desire to rest, this new orientation will produce an energetic warp so great that the person will become feeble. However, he adds that if the person can shrug off this tension, the door is opened to having the most refined cosmological experiences imaginable, making the journey worth the heavy toll.[17] It is conceivable that such events supersede the normal definition of mystical experience and require a new category based on an emerging psychological model.

It is the awareness gained by those who have developed their energy bodies to the artistry and mastery levels, those such as don Juan, that has given rise to modern Toltec philosophy. It has been derived from highly sophisticated reflection and projection, all aimed toward the goal of liberating perception beyond those very embankments.

6

The Nature of
Fundamentalism

Fundamentalism is a type of thinking with definite characteristics regardless of the context in which it occurs. It is a type of cohesion, a type of conditional energy field. When a number of facts are logically woven together a picture of the world emerges, which might be a concept, theory, or entire worldview. For the picture to be useful, it needs to have a boundary, whether the size of its frame is vast or small. Thus the aspect of perception that closes off a viewpoint is vital.

Each stage of development reflects a new baseline, a new picture of the world. At the beginning of a stage, the next stage is foreign. Time and training are needed to elevate the baseline through altered and discrete altered states until major shifts of cohesion occur, such as realizing the world is not flat after all, or that the world is first and foremost comprised of energy.

This is all well and good. But when the picture is not only closed off but also placed inside an unventilated box, difficulties with learning and imagination occur. If we dismiss awareness found in a more expansive or higher-order model in terms of a smaller picture, then we are actively suppressing the new point of view. We are forcing all information to abide by the logic of the status quo. An interesting example can be found regarding the Eastern concept of qi, for which mainstream Western culture does not have an equivalent term.[1] As a result we may abruptly dismiss the existence of an energetic life force. To avoid this difficulty, we need to include flow, movement, openness, and discernment along with closing off. Otherwise we only reflect upon what is already known and do not grow.

CONDITIONAL ENERGY FIELDS

When you are locked in a specific cohesion, you can't see anything beyond the conditions that formed it. It is as though you reside in a world of mirrors, and models aptly illustrate this dynamic. A model defines what is under examination and what the parameters of accepted perception are. It also defines the interpretations and results. This applies to whether you're focusing on an experiment, a religious theme, or an entire worldview. The world of mirrors that both created the model and was created by it can tie perception into a little ball or point the way to unveiling more of the universe. If the mirrors don't let in light from other cohesions, other models, other worlds, or simply new altered states, then you are at the root of fundamentalism.

As a result, your conditional field causes you to bend that which is being experienced into a preexisting arrangement. The field then prevents you from listening, recognizing, and adapting to new data and relationships with the world. And it engenders castigation of those who may challenge the model, be it large or small, as any challenge to the prevailing dogma is seen as heresy. The life of Galileo serves as an example; he spent the latter part of his life under house arrest for simply calling attention to facts that lay outside the accepted version of reality. So it is important to learn how to use models, not be used by them.

Like the ancient mariners of Homer's day who either succumbed to or sailed free from the seductive and treacherous sirens, everyone who makes the voyage of infinity will find themselves having to navigate the world of mirrors. There simply is no other choice. The stages of ontological development offer channel markers to guide awareness through this world, to groom and focus consciousness rather than to close it off.

CLOSURE

Closure, a natural effect of a conditional field, is a force to be reckoned with. *The Law of Closure* found in psychology pertains to defining, refining, eliminating, and consolidating perception.[2] The study of reading, for example, has shown that if a group of people is presented with a paragraph that has one word blanked out, most people will read the paragraph and automatically insert a word, then swear there was no blank spot. In the same manner, a person will interpret what is heard in keeping with his or her own thoughts, even though what is being said might mean something entirely different.

This magnifies to a point where we regard the human world as the essence of the universe rather than a part of it. People *anthropomorphize* reality by giving human traits to elements of nature, God, or anything else. The social world then becomes the principal navigational tool rather than the call of the great beyond. This effect of arranging perception limits the number of external emanations that can be tapped, which, in turn, prevents everyone from becoming more aware. As a result, we collapse the sea of infinity in which we sail into something convenient, perhaps even trivial.

This also serves to illustrate what happens when the unconscious begins to surface. The property of closure causes our conscious awareness to either disregard new perceptions or place them in a known category. The effect is the same: the conscious domain remains static. The good thing about this is that our energy bodies don't explode due to an overload of awareness rushing in. The downside is not recognizing more of our natural heritage.

The contrast between *science* and *scientism* serves to illustrate the benefits and drawbacks of the open-close dynamic of awareness. Science is based on a rigorous method of inquiry. Scientism reflects consensual activities where thoughts about scientific knowledge are given more weight than the actual method that brought about the knowledge. Awareness and understanding from scientific endeavors change all the time, with new knowledge replacing what has come before. Scientism occurs when scientists no longer extend scientific considerations to all areas of inquiry and either remain locked in a previous model or try to force data into an inappropriate model; the door to true investigation then closes.

For example, a novel therapeutic agent that has been shown to produce results in treating a disease may not pass laboratory analysis because the model being used to test efficacy relies on looking only at biological pathways used by the current class of drugs. But the new therapeutic agent might work completely differently from what has come before. If the requirements that the new drug must face before approval inherently discounts their effects, the drug may never see the light of day. The evolution of models needs to go hand-in-hand with discovery.

In respect to bioenergetics, mystical experience, or a more extensive human anatomy, it is not that science is incapable of tackling the related issues; it is that a sufficient number of scientists have not yet completely recognized and defined new areas to explore. These areas are therefore often relegated to philosophy, the fringes of scientific endeavor, or the ranting of pop culture. The same applies to all behavior. Educators, for instance, can ask people to learn and accept the same, unchallenged norms or they can provide the essentials to enable individuals and groups to actively learn. What those essentials might be is a matter of style and method.

In and of itself, the scientific method is an amazingly powerful tool. But it is a tool wielded by humans. In essence, it represents objectivity. In practice, results are biased by what is currently held to be scientific. Data acquisition through cornerstones of perception other than reason is not even considered. Examining its practice therefore well illustrates the consequences of carrying too rigid a viewpoint.

Optimally, scientific models provide a means for objective determinations to account for new data and new revelations about the world. As interpretations directly hinge on cohesion, two people could read or observe the same data yet arrive at completely different meanings. The method has to be applied before it yields results, and the type of results hinge on the level of skill—with the interplay of learning and imagination defining the level.

For good and ill, closure is accentuated by group consensus, which lends mass and momentum. Simple rules of physics demonstrate that the inertia of a larger body makes it more difficult to change path. They form the basis of a bioenergetic interpretation of why cultures often die; they are unable to change quickly enough to avoid natural disaster, war, atmospheric and weather conditions, or whatever else arises. Conversely, in his book *Integral Health,* physician Elliot Dacher points the way to a culture steeped in wisdom, one that takes advantage of what has been learned before yet remains open to whatever waits. The result, he says, is human flourishing.[3]

While closure is required to consolidate gains of learning and essential for the application of knowledge, the trick is to remain open in the midst of tying off what is known. Imagination provides this relief. Overall, learning is a complex binary process of opening and closing awareness that leads to the integration of perceptions. You need to not only take stock in your conscious, known world but also actively cultivate your unconscious, unknown world. The best models therefore incorporate not only the pieces of the picture in question but also openness to new information. In such a manner, you suspend closure and set the stage to make the unconscious more conscious.

FUNDAMENTALISM

When applied to groups, excessive closure—the product of a rigid conditional field—equates with fundamentalism. Fundamentalism can be quiet or loud. It can take the form of professionals who refuse to hear new perspectives just because they think their authority bestows the correct answer, so a wrong medical diagnosis is made or a bridge collapses. It can be a rabble-rouser inciting others to conform to some type of thought or behavior, leading scores of people who are caught in a current of emotion to follow a make-believe flag. As a result of this type of closure a vast amount of misinformation is held as truth by a group consciousness. This is truly where the individual must be able to stand alone. Navigating such travails is an inherent part of the journey to self-actualization.

Whether the fundamentalist cohesion is based on intricacy of reason or emotion, the routines and rituals by which it is formed cement its unquestioned acceptance. We can think of it as a "house" of cohesion, with walls, windows, flooring, carpet, and so on. Various industries facilitated production and distribution of each element, particular cultural values spawned its architecture, and so on. When they are all put together in one construction, the complexity and power of the cohesion is immense. A person can get so fascinated by logic and its interlocking structures that he gets lost in it. Or a person may come to believe the rote beliefs of a philosophy without taking time to measure its effects other than it offers participation within a group. Social acceptance is, after all, is one of our key motivators.[4]

At the heart of fundamentalism is common understanding, which is also the very thing that produces significant gains. Perhaps the dividing line is the institutionalized thinking that calcifies thought and behavior. It becomes the driving force that determines values rather than a template for encouraging learning. A point of view may make sense and so no one wants to relinquish it; people become unwilling to entertain new states of consciousness, especially if doing so might make their current view obsolete. When this is backed by group consensus, the power magnifies. While collective knowledge can significantly add quality for the individual, the downside occurs when individuals surrender their autonomy to the group, forgetting that individual independence enables a group to flourish. Moreover, the bigger the impending changes to an established norm, the greater is the resistance to making the changes; the energy of inertia at work.

Political scientists refer to a *mobilization of bias* when organizations actively promote fundamentalist ideas by requiring a "nondecision" for people to remain in compliance with dogma.[5] In such a setting people cannot stray from the fold through genuine inquiry or by entertaining answers that lie outside the organization's doctrine. This type of entrainment also applies to individuals who try to unduly influence the perception of others by using a prevailing bias to restrict the flow of information. Unchecked, fundamentalism leads to tyranny and signifies estrangement from your core.

When a group is effectively held together by moral self-righteousness, then others need to beware the tide of emotion that follows. The values comprising a fundamentalist stance help generate such responses. As neuroscientist and Nobel Laureate Gerald Edelman points out, "emotions are complex states arising from core interactions with value systems."[6] The complexity forms cohesion. Cohesion then dominates the person rather than the person managing cohesion.

Any cohesive alternative lifestyle has great power, enough to lead its adherents away from convention. Whether it is a cult, a corporation, an intentional community centered on shared values, or a metaphysical path, the adherents of any social group develop some version of a shared conditional energy field. In the same manner, participants within mainstream society develop a conditional field. In general, then, a gathering of like-minded people generates a force—sometimes for better, sometimes for worse.

The "better" aspect is that a group can usually explore aspects of the unknown and accumulate knowledge faster than one person alone. The "worse" aspect is that the shared understanding that comes from these explorations may be misconstrued as being true reality. Whether this distortion comes from scientists, religious leaders, or philosophers, it is fundamentalism. Indeed, whenever there is an attempt to define, confine, or otherwise limit awareness—whenever a step is taken away from potential—that is fundamentalism.

A NATURAL ENERGY FIELD

It is important for individuals to give their best to others and to life. This can't be done in a fundamentalist context. When you cut yourself off from infinity, you diminish your essential relationship to life. Your best comes from new relationships based on opening to potential, and then collapsing that new awareness into a practical framework to make the collective more conscious. At the level of *being*—produced by a natural field—your awareness paradoxically remains open, yet is sufficiently closed to enable you to lead an orderly life. Even grocery shopping requires order and therefore a degree of closure. It is when the stream of consciousness is closed too tightly that growth is hampered.

From the perspective of energetic anatomy, all of this is quite natural. Humans have biologic closed electrical circuits. These are needed for the body to function. Humans also have open circuits such as the chakra network that not only nourish the physical body but also connect us with other spheres and dimensions of energy. From a quantum view, all energy is connected at some level, so even "closed" circuitry is open and in some way influences and is influenced by other energies. The electrical circuitry in your home, for example, generates an electromagnetic field that in some way affects your environment and can be affected by the environment such as an electrical storm.

Fundamentalism may occur at any stage of growth. Whether you are an apprentice or craftsperson, your energy field is conditional. It isn't until you break into the artisan stage that the influence of this type of energy is reduced. And even if you've groomed a natural energy field, you still need to beware of losing yourself in your personal thoughts about the world.

An example of achieving the correct balance of openness and structure can be seen in Maslow's attitude toward the term "ontopsychology," which was coined to signify a new area of investigation relating to *being*. He expressed his hope that the new field was a true expansion of psychology, not an "ism" that would eventually turn into antiscience.[7] By that time in his life, he had grown beyond the field of psychology he fathered. He was more interested in the spiritual dimension of human existence, "spiritual" in the sense of participation with creation and not necessarily having religious connotations.

NEW AGE PHILOSOPHY

Fundamentalism can strike any person or any group, lay or professional. I singled out the practice of science because it is so ingrained and influential in modern life yet its internal politics are not that widely known. In a discussion of the pros and cons of fundamentalism, another force deserves recognition: the pop mysticism culture known as *New Age*. Over recent decades this movement has commanded significant attention, money, and resources. It has become an industry in its own right and continues to influence cultural values. During the mid- to late 1960s, this movement allowed the popular media to bring awareness of chakras and meridians into view. Acupuncture has since been established as part of Western CAM, and chakras are under close scrutiny. The once esoteric knowledge of ancient mysticisms continues to find expression in modern times.

The main thrust of the New Age movement, a renaissance of thought and experience, centers on awakening spirituality. It includes investigations of past lives, meditation, healing, and new relationships with God, just to name a few items on the agenda. Yet, much of this "new" agenda has already been very well established for centuries in philosophies around the world. To a large degree the so-called discoveries are simply reflections of pieces of metaphysical traditions. Perhaps what makes them new is the amount of attention given to them and the numbers of people who are involved. If this is true, the New Age movement could be considered a result of changes in the energy body's uniformity. As previously mentioned, the energy body may be evolving into a more spherical shape. If so, this would lend itself to more people perceiving a more holistic world. And holistic thinking is also very much part of the New Age.

Like metaphysical philosophies, New Age thought is far-reaching and often touches every aspect of a person's life. Since in some ways it could also be considered an umbrella for all metaphysical philosophies, it carries immense power. However, New Age thought is still just another social arrangement, a conditional field based on an inherited set of assumptions about reality, rather than being an ongoing reexamination of our lot as humans. While New Age thinking does provide some direction and offers ways to proceed, it is of finite form and is therefore not the pure art of navigating infinite potential.

Metaphysical philosophies deal with the underlying structures of reality, and New Age considerations only skim the surface. Understanding the difference between occult and mystical makes all the difference in what is experienced. While this movement has provided the service of bringing more ideas to the light of day, the new age quickly gets old when the awakening to new ideas turns to dogma and cultish, occult behavior. Whether your involvement is with the classic traditions or New Age pursuits, be careful, as you may think you've got it all straight when you really don't.

EXAMPLES OF FUNDAMENTALISM

When you are able to talk the lingo of a system, and things start making sense, it can be very seductive. To avoid the pitfalls of fundamentalism, it is necessary to accept the legitimacy of other points of view, especially if they conflict with yours. The universe is a wide-open place. Why confine it to your pet thoughts? If you let go and constantly challenge your assumptions, your thoughts will change.

To avoid getting caught in fundamentalism, it is also helpful to closely examine the precepts of any system. A close look at some of the slogans and tips popular in the New Age movement and traditional metaphysical philosophies can be very instructive.

The world is an illusion. Yes, it is an illusion in relation to other points of view. But using the model of cohesion and the focal point, we could also say that everything is real. Whenever cohesion is formulated and a focal point position is stabilized, that is what makes one thing "real," and everything else an illusion. But any focal point position, whether for an individual or a group, is an illusion when you compare it with infinite potential. Still, that thought stems from a focal point position, which makes it real.

There are no mistakes. This perspective definitely opens you up to potential, knowing that there is perfection in each and every event that occurs, but take a hard look. You've never made a true mistake? This doesn't mean you can't learn from your mistakes, and thereby make something good out of them. But learning is limited when you think you never make a mistake.

You create your own reality. This is a popular expression. But maybe the impact of this slogan is limited. It is a philosophical assumption based on a Western perspective of having free will. It is not necessarily fact, even though we think we can see it working in our lives when we examine the effects of our actions based on a free-will model.

A slogan only holds sway if you use it consistently and take it seriously, not just when it's convenient. If you fully accept that you create your reality, you have to assume responsibility for everything in your life, including your neighbors and how they impact you. This doesn't mean you are responsible for your neighbors; it means you are responsible for having those neighbors in your life. In this manner, you unveil deeper levels of yourself. By going deeper and deeper, you come to your core; you get to a point where you no longer interpret or define the world, such as by saying "you create your own reality."

A counterpoint is that perhaps the pressure from cosmic emanations on our energy bodies generates our decisions. In other words, maybe a decision occurs by acquiescing to a force that forms cohesion. But since we've learned to develop reason over other modes of perception, we conjure up the perception that somehow we are the ones really making the decisions.

Earth is a school. There's no doubt that learning takes place in humans. Exactly what is learned may be open to question, but humans learn. In general, what is learned is more and more about the human condition, and not necessarily from a grand viewpoint. Therefore, by saying "Earth is a school" is projection based on the natural tendency to learn. In so doing, we make our environment a place of learning. But what life is, what it really is, and what it really is for, is a mystery dwelling in the depths of infinity. To view it otherwise locks the door to potential.

It was supposed to happen. Says who?

There's a reason for everything. Sure, you can find a reason for anything, but that doesn't mean that there *is* a reason for it. To have "a reason for it," to find meaning, requires relating the experience to a specific logic or to a worldview. If this is done enough it will build a conditional energy field. One field might lead you to reason that you are adept at mathematics because you have genetic makeup that lends itself to math. Another field might lead you to think you are adept at mathematics because you have good karma from a past life. Genetic makeup then follows having good karma. This enhanced accountability is what makes New Age fundamentalism so difficult to overcome. Being able to account for more leads to the belief that you have the inside angle. As an aspect of closure, humans attribute meaning and value to their thoughts about what the universe is.

We live in a world of duality. Yes, we do. Maybe this is because we have a two-sided horizontal brain: the right and left hemispheres. We project the innate tendencies of our hardwiring onto the external world: the world becomes dualistic because of the way information is regulated and processed by the brain.

The brain's structure also makes it clear why Toltecs say there are three energy fields. Remember that in addition to right and left partitioning, there is a three-level, vertical partitioning relating to physical, emotional, and abstract-mental functions. These vertical segments easily correspond to the first, second, and third energy fields. Perhaps the interplay between the horizontal and vertical areas of the brain is what produces new models of reality, such as it being multidimensional.

As you develop the stages of awakening a dualistic world of good and evil evolves into an interpretation of things being positive or negative. Eventually you see that your perception of the world is a state of mind.[8]

FREE WILL?

The concept of free will offers a good example of how an idea often turns into dogmatic thinking, able to start arguments, if not wars, when people dig into their viewpoints and build cosmologies around them. The philosophical differences about whether humans have free will can well illustrate the value of taking the time to look at other perspectives.

A major aspect of many religions addresses this very point. Eastern philosophies are known to espouse the nonexistence of free will, whereas the Western mind-set typically contends that free will is part and parcel of human existence. Whichever viewpoint is valued, the perceptions relating to it are rooted in the inherent capacity of humans to form subject-object relationships. Humans are able to examine their condition and ask questions such as, "If we have free will, what is its capacity? How much choice do we have?" Perhaps the question may be better stated as "Why don't we choose to act in ways that don't harm ourselves, others, or the environment—especially when we know our actions are causing harm?"

The notion of free will addresses fundamental, universal aspects of being human. It requires looking at individuals as unique, as being able to discern and move independently of the group. It carries that much meaning. In traditional Buddhist thought, for instance, free will doesn't exist simply because there is no self to have free will. Even some cognitive scientists hold fast to this view.[9] On the other hand, free will is very much a part of Christian traditions. The idea of sin is at times viewed as straying from the path, and *reconciliation* is placing oneself back in a proper relationship with God.[10] Choice, after all, or the ability to find redemption, is derived from the notion that we have options to select from, and the power to enact that choice.

Arriving at either understanding requires an intense effort of consolidating a number of seemingly disparate pieces of logic into a unified whole, a task no different from any other learning. The point here is that classic traditions expound particular points of view that have easily withstood the test of time. That is both a blessing and curse.

Jung maintains that *will* implies having enough energy to act independently of instinct, yet the motivation of *will* is essentially biological and therefore instinctual.[11] From Maslow's perspective, free choice typically doesn't enter the picture until a person expresses self-actualizing behavior. The hierarchy he articulated of deficit and growth needs speaks directly to this.[12] If a person is governed by need, how much latitude for choice does he or she have?

As part of having no free will, we might regard our destiny as being fixed in place, and see all time as occurring within a single instant, with the rest being a magnificent play of perception of moving through what we call time-space. At the same time, we could use this high-end perspective to support free will. Both models enable awareness. The machinery of logic to do so is just different. And so the resulting form of *being* conscious is different.

In his book, *Psychology of Religion,* scholar Paul Johnson argues that choice is evident when one is more conscious.[13] The energy body schematic offers a look at what becoming conscious might actually entail. From an energetic standpoint, however, perhaps inertia governs all of our behavior and free will is an illusion generated from a sense of movement. Learning allows one to change inertia, but was the learning itself a product of inertia? Isn't most learning, at least in the early years of life, based on participating in a given reality? Free will, from this perspective, is just buying what's being sold.

The synthesis of these two ends of the free will, where free-will spectrum may not necessarily be a blending of models but the evolution to yet another model; the effect of a Hegelian dialectic, if you will, where thesis and antithesis collide to create a new synthesis. In this example, the growth may be that of ontological intelligence—the full scope of awareness—where the next answer, and the next choice, is found in the enactment of higher order logic.

According to the Toltec worldview, emanations carry commands. There is a command that humans must eat and that humans must engage in self-reflection. How the command is carried out, though, seems open to interpretation and decision-making. Choice then originates from completely surrendering yourself to an emanation to step outside of it.[14] By absorbing the energy of a certain level of consciousness, you open yourself to yet another influence. While you may lose a sense of choice in the new emanation, you've gained at least some freedom, and therefore some choice, resulting from having become more conscious of the prior emanation.

The further you integrate the human world, meaning the more you command human-world emanations, the more you step into worlds beyond your current imagination; after all, we are multidimensional creatures living in a multidimensional creation. Your choice then becomes aligning with, or entraining to, particular emanations of the human or cosmic worlds. All major religions and spiritual philosophies offer the possibility of such ability.

Both camps and everything in between can conjure up some pretty fancy footwork and we haven't even scratched the surface. One way or other, the belief you hold about the issue results from your entrainment to a line of thought, an emanation of intellectual energy. "No free will" supports behaving in line with the properties of energy where at a certain level all behavior has already been decided. "Free will" offers a connection with energy fields that enable this thing called "choice." Any way you look at it, it is all part of infinity's dance. And within infinity, everything is occurring—including the legitimacy of all philosophical assumptions about infinity.

MANAGING FUNDAMENTALISM

Fundamentalism is a powerful force of entrainment. This force can be managed and transcended, which is part of ontological development. There's no doubt that the fundamentals—the essential basics—of a system serve to help liberate perception. They keep you heading toward your destination and make the journey the essence of your life. It's only when you lose yourself in the fundamentals that you go astray. Here are some suggestions that may help you navigate infinity:

1. Don't use your knowledge as an excuse not to look at yourself.
2. Learn to *see*, as doing so suspends conditional fields.
3. Shift your focal point regularly. Fundamentalists try to maintain a certain perspective, and this means maintaining a particular focal-point position.
4. Cultivate a bent for examination, for understanding. Toltecs have called this *sobriety* and hold that it automatically leads to a shift in the focal point.[15]
5. Challenge all of the assumptions that make up your worldview.
6. Don't let your love for the fundamentals turn you into a fundamentalist.
7. Don't confuse intellectual fluency with having the ability to do what it is you are talking about.
8. Realize that just because you have had an experience—like a NDE—doesn't mean you now know.
9. Get comfortable with not knowing anything. Then open yourself to knowing. Repeat as needed.

Millions of people are being exposed to, and influenced by, fundamentalist thinking, be they scientists, religious zealots, hardcore New Agers, or whatever. When many people adopt a new pattern of thought, it results in a revolution. The communist, socialist, industrial, evangelical, and green movements are all examples, as is the Inquisition. At its face value, a revolution is neither good nor bad. The measure of its value is its effect on the consciousness and development of individuals and groups.

Yet, for the revolutionary transformation of freedom, even this power must be transcended. Supplanting one template of thought with another is not a recipe for complete evolution. All too often when people have authority in one field, they assume they have authority in others. On top of this, people construct many interpretations of what they think is occurring rather than examine what actually is occurring.

If there were a technology that could accurately indicate how much of the energy body had become conscious, we would have a way to predict any person's level of fundamentalism. Seen from a behavioral psychological perspective, that would translate to hard data that could be used to predict behavior. From a transpersonal perspective, it would make the assessment of ontological development possible. We could then map practically any dysfunction and create therapies, all based on the perspective that humans have objective, quantifiable energy bodies.

EVALUATING A PHILOSOPHY

Unless you are somehow gifted, to firmly move forward in learning you need a system that will offer you an enlarged worldview, channel markers to keep you on track, and how-to-do-it skills. This is exactly what metaphysical philosophies and science offer. The markers provided may be simple tips. For example, don Juan advised Castaneda not to become overconfident, as Toltec practices can be deadly. This is backed up with traditional scientific research. Psychiatrist Arthur Deikman, in his landmark study of cult behavior, *The Wrong Way Home,* found that overconfidence leads to the demise of spiritual organizations as well as individuals.[16]

A philosophy provides a framework that can help you in the process of letting your current knowledge become obsolete as you develop a new set of perspectives. Part of the challenge is to remain true to a philosophy while also remaining true to yourself. In this light, a viable philosophy always has two features that indicate whether it's strong enough, and flexible enough, to get you to your core—the overriding consideration of developing your energy body.

The first indicator of a viable system is that it's nonexclusive. Ideas, practices, procedures, worldviews, and goals are open to all. Whether its practitioners actually follow the path they preach about is another story. That's a fight that takes place within the person.

Deikman found that self-righteousness is a marked feature of cult members. You've found your way and that's that . . . often resulting in great suffering for those around you. Embarking on such a path may only lead into room after room of mirror images of yourself, or rather of the images you have of yourself. This is often accompanied by the attitude that group membership is the be-all and end-all; this is often taken to a level of criticizing if not ostracizing others. Another indication of cult behavior is the attitude that there is only one path and perhaps there are only a chosen few who may follow it. Deikman found that devaluing outsiders was a firm indication of cult activity.[17]

The second indicator of a viable system is that the philosophy clearly teaches that it is only a means to an end. It is to help generate clarity, not lock perception within its grand scheme. Author John Van Auken has observed that phenomena, or the imaginings of a worldview, can blind one to the greater realms of existence or can serve as a bridge to them.[18] Having fun with *psi,* OBEs, NDEs, and mystical experiences may open the way to a greater sense and vision of the world. On the other hand, such experiences may lead you to think that they *are* the world and to become so enthralled with your discoveries that you forget about further development.

A doctrine or system—of metaphysical, scientific, or other persuasion —represents the articulation of craftsmanship. This becomes a group's baseline consciousness. Like any other baseline, the orientation, terminology, understanding, and skills of enactment change over time. Part of the craft of a high-value system is that it helps you continually expand your boundaries. For the individual or the collective, remaining at the level of craftsmanship is an invitation for the craft to become fundamentalism. The selective cueing of the path needs to point the way to artistry if not mastery and, in so doing, connect you with infinity. Otherwise dogma and possibly cult behavior arise.

In fundamentalism, instead of closure serving to support learning, the work of learning is turned into acts of closure. As members of the flock, fundamentalists find meaning within group understanding. On the other hand, an artisan or master finds meaning by matching personal energies with pure potential, and then letting life unfold from there. From this relationship, each and every step of life is a renewal, not a repetition of form.

7

A Creative Life

Creativity, or bringing something into being, results from the interaction between form and potential. Form is cohesion, a type of energy field. Potential is abstract energy; that is, energy that has possibilities of realization but isn't there yet. Pure potential is completely abstract, the infinite creation, which contains everything but has no form.

How these energies play together determines what is created—the imaginings of your life and world. Remember that whatever occurs reflects your cohesion, or rather the capacity of your cohesion to perceive it. Cohesion also determines how you continue to connect with potential, which influences what you create as the energy body meets greater emanations.

If you don't connect with potential, you will just be circling within the conditional field you already have. This may keep you amused, but you are not going to grow very much. When you squarely face potential, you place your life on the line—each and every moment of it. This will move you from talk about life into a relationship with the world in which you live to the hilt. The following perspectives will serve to help you to orient awareness and gauge how you wish to build your life.

DISCOVERY

Part of creativity is discovery, which can take many forms. There is the brilliant flash of intuition, when all effort suddenly comes together to deliver an expanded knowing. This *Eureka!* mode of invention has been a mainstay since humans became conscious and curious.

Another form of discovery is serendipity, the seemingly accidental or chance discovery. When Alexander Fleming noticed that bacteria were not growing around the mold that had appeared on some unwashed culture plates he had casually left on his lab bench, he turned that observation into penicillin.

There is the time-honored plodding of a disciplined mind, as it wrestles with what is known, what it sees that doesn't fit the known, and eventually illuminates that which waits behind the veil. Einstein remained on track for years as he cultivated the thinking that eventually led to his theory of relativity. The simple truth is that the heart of discovery contains many styles, these and others, and that each supports the other.

Discovery is regulated by models (points of view), which at once open and close perception. All of the different avenues of discovery are constructs that allow us to focus awareness in ways that deliver results. Even serendipity, where discovery-by-chance may seem random, needs the support of a context in which the discovery may take hold. Fleming, for example, had an extensive scientific background that guided the application of his observation; penicillin didn't surface from a void. At the same time, discovery also requires a suspension of what is thought to be true—a form of deautomatization—to allow imagination to come forth.

Creativity results from the interplay between learning and imagination. For example, the wildly commercial success of the previously unknown "pet rock" was based on the known commodities of "pet" and "rock." Placing the two together was new but not foreign. Likewise, it took some time before the idea of a submarine became a concept worth developing, and then it took longer still to make it actually work.

Perception can be closed when data consistent with a new and wider view is not even recognized or is simply dismissed as irrelevant. The person advancing the ideas is often castigated or worse by those who, for whatever reason, have a stake in the current scheme of things. Even in the midst of the technological development of undersea travel, in which supposedly foolish ideas were becoming reality, the mere talk of something that could fly in the sky would have almost ensured a hard rebuff; the prevailing model regarding the impossibility of air travel inhibited forward movement.

The process of discovery is like being part of a motion picture set that is so well designed that there is an implicit assumption about its reality. Then the curtain lifts, revealing yet a new landscape and people say, "Oh, great, now we are at the real world." This happens time and again as human knowledge increases, yet we are not taught that the curtain will rise once again to reveal yet another entirely new vista. Going backstage to observe what actually occurs, rather than remaining focused on the special effects, is also at the heart of creativity.

INTELLIGENCE

A defining aspect of discovery is intelligence, resources you bring to bear on a situation, as well as the means with which you apply them. Intelligence is often directly related to a score, an intelligence quotient, commonly known as *IQ*. In recent years, this has been challenged as being a very limited perspective on human capabilities. Some say the measurement of IQ is culturally biased, others say it focuses too much on intellectual capacities, and still others say it's just plain obsolete.

In fact, research indicates that intelligence surfaces in many ways. In addition to Goleman's emotional intelligence (EQ),[1] educator and cognitive scientist Howard Gardner provides evidence in his classic book, *Frames of Mind: The Theory of Multiple Intelligences,* that humans have within themselves a number of different intelligences. He says "human beings have evolved to exhibit several intelligences and not to draw variously on one flexible intelligence." Included among the various intelligences that Gardner says we have are those of language, mathematics, music, the physical body, and social adeptness. He even suggests that there is a *spiritual* intelligence.[2] Plus, each chakra contains its own intelligence, as do each of the cornerstones of perception.

Intelligence can be defined as "the ability to meet and adapt to novel situations; the ability to utilize abstract concepts effectively; and the ability to grasp relationships and to learn quickly."[3] Gardner defines intelligence as the ability "to resolve genuine problems or difficulties." He adds, "possession of an intelligence is most accurately thought of as a *potential*" [italics mine].[4] Pure potential, then, is pure intelligence. It embodies all forms of intelligence, all waiting to be tapped in a variety of ways, to thereby engender creativity.

Intelligence is our ability to open to potential, to apply what is perceived, and to integrate the results. This profile of intelligence may then be applied to whatever situation is at hand, whether it is working with mathematics, composing music, *seeing,* or dipping into social psychology. Since evolving the energy body relies on intersecting with emanations, with a greater potential of energy, with awakening new cohesions and then applying these results, intelligence may also be thought of as the ability to manage cohesion. Accordingly, plugging into potential is intelligent. Evolving through your energy body is intelligent. Bringing yourself to life is intelligent.

ETHICS

A key aspect of intelligence is the ethic behind it. Ethics are governing principles of behavior: values, morals, rules. They change over time and the considerations associated with ethical standards—including religious, cultural, professional, and personal values—are vast. Ethics has become a well-developed line of inquiry with highly specialized divisions such as *deontological,* or rules and principles, and *teleological,* or examination of behavior based on the purpose or end result. New areas are also emerging. *Human nature* ethical inquiry, for example, presupposes that behavior should be measured in line with how it affects personal development.[5]

Individual and social ethics are foundations of intelligent, if not creative, behavior. There are no set answers; even centuries-old religious dogmas change. There are, though, bits and pieces to be considered in light of the energy-body model, where ethics influence cohesion and represent growth toward core. As food for thought, some of these considerations follow.

Compassion

Compassion may be defined as "deep awareness of the suffering of another coupled with the wish to relieve it."[6] Holding to this definition, Toltecs do not have compassion. They may be able to empathize with or understand another's plight. They may be able to apply a lesson found in another's misfortune to their own lives, thereby avoiding the same trouble. They may render assistance. But they won't think that other people are so powerless that they have to be coddled. They won't think the other person has to be changed, shown the light, or saved. The best of Toltecs have been born, says don Juan, from squalor. We all have the means to command our lives, he maintains, and there is nothing to change in anyone.[7]

Being overly compassionate diminishes objectivity. The concern given to a situation can reduce your ability to assess the *meta*problem. That is, you have increased difficulty seeing the underlying problem that is causing the personal distress, rendering you unable to take effective action to produce a long-lasting remedy. This is why some Toltecs strive not to care. This doesn't mean they are blasé or callous. And it certainly doesn't mean they lack gusto. It means that they are striving for a level of objectivity to be able to act precisely and effectively. They are cultivating the keen indifference that will allow them to be successful.[8] Some may think this view is horrendous. But it doesn't mean Toltecs can't be kind. In fact, don Juan says that kindness is required to balance wisdom.[9]

Judgment

Judgment is a form of closure. It stems from interpretation and locks you into a particular emotional and mental disposition. Even at its best, judgment keeps you locked in the throes of fundamentalism. You may even want to physically attack others.

Judgment removes you from potential. It requires that you constantly justify your high-horse attitude, and so it requires you to work overtime to maintain that manner of self-reflection. Plus, what is ethical in one culture may not be in another. What is held sacred by some cultures may be heresy to others, even though people in both strive to do good deeds. Judgment can therefore be simply oppressive when one person or group ridicules another.

Being nonjudgmental doesn't mean you can't be highly discerning. It doesn't mean you aren't allowed to take steps to avoid difficulties or rectify injustices and unlawful acts. It means giving freedom to the world to be as it is and to be more objective about yourself. From this stance, it permits the understanding that promotes positive change rather than ongoing strife. From yet another angle, it offers support to awaken your energy body.

Forgiveness

Forgiveness of the transgressions of self and others offers a release of the focal point, a release of a cohesion bound by judgment. But it doesn't mean being a whipping boy. It is a relaxation of tension that opens you to growth simply by ceasing to expend all the energy required to maintain a nonforgiving posture. In *Why Forgive?* author Johann Christoph Arnold provides stories of the sojourns to forgiveness by various people that demonstrate why forgiveness is important.[10] They clearly show that forgiveness enables us to free ourselves from the emotional debilitation of being tied down by bitterness, heal the emotional and physical disorders caused by the lack of forgiveness, and restore our relationship with God.

Power and Control

The manner in which you exercise control over yourself, others, and the environment makes all the difference in your life. The more control you have over your energy body, the more ability you have to actively mold your world. This is why control is one of the barriers to ontological development. It is hard not to want to control your world. You may even want to be compassionate; to change things for the better, but both can lead you to become a dictator. The effects of control on behavior are very sneaky.

At the craftsmanship stage, when *will* is pulled from its dormancy, you can modify your circumstances by aligning with emanations of your choosing. As a result, the many forms of personal desire can tug at your sensibilities. As a corrective, don Juan says that it is a shame to align with the human world and forget that the focal point is an essential quality of being human, but it is even more of a loss to use this knowledge of the focal point for personal gain.[11]

The guiding principle is that knowledge of the energy body is to be used to reach your core, not for control of any other type. Core is the essence of how you are created, and this release to a higher *will,* rather than to desire, is a defining characteristic of modern Toltec ethics. These teachings are rooted in the energy body and so serve as an apt illustration of developing a natural versus contrived relationship with the world. Creating a life based on expression of core is not considered personal desire. At each step, this measurement becomes an intricate and delicate balance.

Toltecs, says don Juan, are like anybody else pursuing a vocation. They can be good or bad. In fact, since they've learned to move their focal points, they can easily injure others. But, he advises, we must move past ordinary considerations. We must be governed by morality and beauty.[12] This involves the development of an ethic based on personal freedom rather than on the accumulation of power. Part of this ethic is the practice of impeccability, which automatically gives others their freedom as well. In fact, don Juan says a person of knowledge—an artisan—would never under any circumstance harm another person.[13]

In practice, you wouldn't *will* an outcome or even test the possibility of being able to do so. And you wouldn't exploit others. When you work with the craft and create a good life, any change that needs to come will come of its own accord. By not using your resources for control, you can develop an exquisite relationship with the world. And, as don Juan says, there will come a time when you have all of your resources and abilities in check, and you will know when and how to use them. By then, you will have become the true artisan.[14]

Love

Love can be approached in many ways and defined in many ways. It can mean leaving things alone or taking action. It can be romantic or platonic, spousal or filial, tough or unconditional. It can be focused on a rock or into the heart of infinity.

Perhaps love is awareness itself, or perhaps it is the feeling of expansion. After all, when we fall in love we usually become more aware and feel as though we are stretching out. We are also more allowing, accepting. As a mode of expansion, love serves to cultivate a natural energy field.

Christian theology is rooted in love. And love is at the center of Hindu Bhakti mysticism.[15] Toltec philosophy, which encourages one to have a "romance with knowledge," or to quest for deep understanding free from bias, also addresses love, citing it as the only thing that offers joy and freedom. It carries so much weight it is something to be enacted in the face of any circumstance.[16]

Don Juan says that Toltec seers *see* love as specific colors representing bandwidths of emanations. These clusters are part of what creates and defines different life forms. Even then, only one of these is of the human domain.[17] But having a limited number of colors doesn't support a worldview in which *everything* is love. Maybe the human aspect of the universe has been anthropomorphized to include everything. Perhaps the Toltec meaning needs to be recast.

In any case, teachings on love are usually found in ethical systems.

Whatever the orientation, love is a major component—perhaps the defining element—in living a conscious life.

Responsibility

His Holiness the Dalai Lama places each individual act in a universal perspective. Two people sharing a well must be mindful of their actions in service to the other; each country needs to recognize that one faltering economy affects other economies around the world; and each driver needs to see that the pollution of one car adds to the destruction of the entire environment.[18] Simply accepting the obvious means that each person carries immense responsibility for self and the whole. It is interesting that quantum entanglement also speaks to the interconnectedness of everything. How this plays out is where the arguments erupt.

Guidance can be found in the entire body of ethics that we participate in, be it religious or secular. Richard Sennett, in *The Corrosion of Character,* cites how the environment, in the case of the workplace, shapes personal responsibility. Often one ethic may be stated as part of the corporate culture but the forces within produce a different effect, taking personal and societal tolls. In turn, he cites a weakening of character in the modern workplace where people renounce accountability.[19]

Personal responsibility is where the rubber hits the road in the journey toward infinity. It is your immediate connection to your life and those about you. It is the driving force of building a life. Responsibility, as an example of Toltec ethic, means that you are ready to die for your actions.[20] That is pretty crisp, clear, and clean. It falls to individual responsibility to summon those resources to reach core.

Character

The sum of all these attributes is a person's character, or ethical strength. Character for Toltecs, as measured by *impeccability,* is the essential ingredient of realizing the stages of awakening. Throughout Castaneda's books, don Juan delivers lessons on a complex style of character marked by saving energy, being deliberate and independent, and constantly stretching into the unknown. According to him, the back-bone of a warrior is marked by humility and efficiency.[21]

Taoism holds fast to *virtue* or "uprightness." This is a perfect attainment of harmony based on the latent, innate power of the individual.[22] Likewise, Maslow regards character as the deepest part of a person. He outlines five character attitudes and says changing any of them changes the person. These attitudes relate to self, significant others, social groups, nature and physical reality, and, for some people, supernatural forces.[23]

A common aspect of these approaches is the quest to find and nurture your own innermost qualities. Whether you call it actualization, individuation, or virtue, the core value of each system is precisely that: core value. That is, ethical behavior emanates from each individual's core. Through finding your place in the world, you can better serve all.

ETHICAL MODELS

Models emerge out of the collective consciousness. Even if inspired by an individual, a model must have some type of relationship to the world outside the individual for it to have pragmatic use. Group consensus is an effect, or perhaps even a use, of the collective awareness. At the same time, don Juan considers group agreements to be "skimming." That is, we forget our constructs are arbitrary arrangements and so consider them to be actual reality.[24] This also applies to creating ethical standards.

There are ethical divisions between the major religions and within each religion. When values clash, so do people. Wars have started over very simple things: the color of skin, the shape of eyes. These days, the topic of abortion often produces a heated environment. "Right to Life" activists have killed "Right to Choose" adherents. That is more than ironic. And mudslinging, arm-waving, and epithet-calling galore can result from putting someone who thinks physician-assisted suicide is ethical in the same room as someone who doesn't.

There is also a growing ethic in some circles that holds high the value of noninterference. People may then avoid taking action in the attempt to let the entire world be free and to allow the infinite to be just that. However, noninterference is often a horrid distortion of deautomatization in which anything is allowed to occur. All too often what has been learned is cast aside. While the effects of global warming on this finite planet are just one experience of an infinite variety of experiences of all creation, we need to be responsible creatures as well as trying to be open.

What is the intrinsic human value of allowing genocide? Perhaps "noninterference" is an innate recognition of the need to avoid the abuse of power that somehow is subverted into something else. Staying locked open seems to be an exotic form of fundamentalism. These concerns make it clear that both the open and closed positions of consciousness are needed for ethical conduct.

The Toltec model is a warrior ethic. Ethics are shaped by the perception that we are in a constant struggle. But the struggle isn't against anything; it is continuous engagement with the barriers that keep us from freedom, from reaching core, and, perchance, from traveling beyond the human dimension.

GROUP CREATIVITY

Led by changes in individual consciousness, the collective consciousness and group consensus gradually expand. What used to be solely in the realm of imagination is learned en masse. Different, if not new, arrangements with reality occur all the time. No matter the form, the arenas to cultivate creativity are immense.

History
Don Juan divides the evolution of Toltec philosophy neatly into the old and new cycles. The old cycle, which brewed for thousands of years, was characterized by abuses of power, bizarre practices of bending human

cohesion into other life forms, and obscure formulas and incantations. He thought that such practices led to destruction.[25]

Between one hundred to five hundred years ago, Toltecs were almost exterminated by the Indian wars and Spanish conquest of Mexico. Their intricate reflection-projection blinded them to the impending environmental threat of invading armies. "They didn't even see it coming," as the saying goes.

In the midst of strife, the remnant of surviving seers went underground and revamped their teachings. Seeing that the prior behaviors had led to a dead end, they produced an ethic in which the real purpose of the craft was to shift the focal point, and do so in a manner that promoted knowledge and freedom. In essence, the old cycle was based on bondage whereas the new cycle wished to exercise potential and, in so doing, revamp the basic options and behaviors concerned with being alive.[26]

The new cycle reckoned that most of the difficulties faced by Toltec seers—old and new cycles alike—stemmed from self-reflection. This is illustrated by a comparison between those who don't have self-restraint versus those who seek practical goals. It is the latter group, maintains don Juan, who resolve the problem of self-reflection and what he refers to as self-importance.[27] Perhaps this is equally attributable to our current course of abuses of political and economic power and of environmental destruction.

It is also possible that those of old cycle were actually living up to their natural field. During that epoch uniformity of the energy body was oblong. As a result, the forms that cohesion could take were limited. The options for behavior could only be expressed in specific directions. Stretching through the energy body for all the best reasons then produced dark aberrations rather than the more holistic, mystical orientation of the new cycle.

Characteristic of this inherent limitation, the old cycle didn't have a penchant for understanding, which is a signature of the new cycle. While Toltec inquiry is quite rigorous, in some ways it is markedly different from modern standards. The accepted modes and means of perception alone highlight this variance. How more of the unconscious is brought to light pertains to style as well as to the ethical standards surrounding such investigations.

A body of ethics is only as good as the fundamental orientation of those producing the ethic. If the ethos isn't derived from core values, the effect is estrangement from essential nature. With the historical reformation, the Toltec quest shifted from creating highly unusual and intricate cohesions to exercise control to tempering cohesion to reach core, develop the artisan stage, and thereby leave the teachings themselves.

Toltecs are not the only people who have gone through such dark times. The Christian Inquisition certainly is an example of a less-than-noble endeavor. Furthermore, a couple thousand years ago, Taoists in China went through an evolution reminiscent of the Toltec experience. Prior to that time Taoists saw themselves as being ruled by a pantheon of gods and they actively sought temporal power. Over time, Taoism became more streamlined, developed pragmatic goals such as being a force behind Traditional Chinese Medicine, and developed into one of the major philosophies of our times.[28]

Environment

It is difficult to be creative if the environment is not suitable. Physicist Milo Wolff points out, "Every charged particle is part of the universe and the universe is part of each charged particle. This implies that each of us, including you and me, are connected together as part of the observable universe!"[29] It has also become increasingly clear that inclusion of the environment is necessary to define anatomy and physiology. Scientific studies, for example, show how conditions such as the degree of lighting affect biochemical reactions and behavior.[30]

Furthermore, in his groundbreaking book, *The Biology of Belief,* cell biologist and medical school professor Bruce Lipton provides a compelling case that challenges current scientific thinking that cellular activity is regulated by genetics. Instead he holds that a cell's life is determined by its physical and energetic environment. Lipton also offers consideration that both of these models result from beliefs, not necessarily from what is actual.[31]

By definition, our connectedness impacts virtually every aspect of our lives. How groups relate to others and to the world is also a determinant of the environment. Moreover, humans have populated Earth to such an extent that our energies are now significantly influencing the cohesion of the planet. This is bioenergetics in motion, the relationship between organisms and the environment.

Self-reflection has an upside and downside regarding the environment. The downside is that projection-reflection blocks awareness; the upside is that it permits accurate assessment. Humans have done a magnificent job of carving out a niche that enhances survival and even allows for leisure time to play, travel, and contemplate. Yet it is this basic relationship that is causing difficulty. We need to take the best of what we know and establish a new relationship—a symbiotic relationship—rather than continue as predators.

From an ethical perspective, global warming and an assortment of other environmental concerns are part and parcel of the ethical issues confronting business. Site selection, emissions, deforestation/reforestation, renewable resources, and economic development are all part of the agenda.[32] In turn, according to Michael Lerner, author of *Spirit Matters,* responding to corporate, as well as individual and social responsibility for all environmental concerns, requires a spiritual assessment and direction. Lerner promotes a "globalization of spirit," where self-interest gives way to awareness and participation in a larger order.[33]

From a psychological view, Maslow points out that the environment of family and culture are absolute requirements for actualization. At the same time, autonomy comes with self-actualization, which results in less fear and anxiety as well as a greater ability to handle environmental situations such as tragedy, stress, and deprivation. A greater independence is generated that allows full individuality but not, Maslow maintains, at the expense of the environment. In fact, the ability to act independently of the environment and to measure your steps by your own sense of responsibility is a defining attribute of psychological health.[34]

As articulated by Lipton, the active field of *epigenetics* deals with how environment, perceptions, and beliefs affect genetic expression.[35] This expression determines what proteins will be produced and so how the body functions. In addition, in illuminating difficulties with experimenter bias—including how experiments are designed, conducted, and interpreted—researchers have recently cited quantum entanglement to explain how a model held by a person participating in an experiment is part of the environment and therefore a determinant of the experiment and its outcome.[36]

Biophysicist James Oschman points out that we live as part of multiple environments. From intracellular chemical communication to electromagnetic fields of power connected to extraterrestrial influences, we exist in a multitude of internal and external environments. Sound, light, and a variety of magnetic and electromagnetic fields are just part of this vast energetic landscape. It is also clear that this energetic environment affects physical health. A cursory look at weather changes and allergies reveals a causal connection between health and environment. Added to this, there is growing concern that human-made, energetic pollution disrupts the normal functions of the body.[37]

Overall, a holistic approach to health requires an assessment of your relationship to your environment. Traditional Chinese Medicine is based on balancing the body with its environment.[38] Homeopathy requires the practitioner to examine environmental factors that may produce, prolong, or maintain a disorder.[39] And Valerie Hunt demonstrates how the environment affects the aura.[40] This is noteworthy as the aura reveals the condition of the whole person but is often affected before the physical body manifests the positive or negative condition reflected in the aura. This means the aura can act as a diagnostic tool.

From a Toltec perspective, the energy body is *seen* as intimately connected with its environment. You are therefore part of all that is around you, seen and unseen. The alignment of outer and inner energies is the basis of perception. When your perceptions change it is due to a change in relation to the environment. Expanding your alignments increases consciousness. This, in turn, leads to tapping an ever-increasing order, resulting from accessing more emanations of energy.[41]

We are immersed in an infinite number of vibrations, says don Juan, and human perception is relegated to a specific bandwidth.[42] But the collective consciousness is expanding as individuals continue to explore recondite areas of consciousness and then express those findings within the whole. As a result, we may be stepping beyond what being human once meant as we awaken more of the energy body as a group.

Technology

An integral part of our environment, technology is the means to channel potential into practical use. No matter if technology is an ancient plow or a space shuttle, it is a creative force that touches practically every aspect of our lives. Technology is considered applied science. Well practiced, science is an adventure into the unknown and technology turns those endeavors into practical gains. From tires to windows to engines and the means to make them, to the thinking behind it all, automobiles alone reflect how deeply technology pervades our lives.

In addition to the material and mechanical varieties, technology also includes cognition. A working technology is evolved from a concept that is pulled out of the unknown and eventually gains conscious acceptance. That is, technology emerges from the human unconscious and the possibilities held within. Our current line of technological development mimics science-fiction technologies. Reason is evolving and becoming more capable of handling out-of-this-world concepts. The notion of stepping on the face of the moon was once only found in an entertaining story. While it will take time for humans to build a flying saucer, teleportation of quantum matter is already occurring.[43] New scientific theories that change the landscape of what is considered possible are rapidly emerging. As a result, group consensus about reality will invariably change and, in time, children will be raised with a completely new baseline state of consciousness.

As material technology is based in reason, it represents constructs emanating from personal and group projection. A metaphysical system offers techniques for implementing and actually developing the worldview it espouses, where the emphasis is on innate ways and means to develop awareness and knowing.[44] This can be seen in Toltec teachings, which render a mechanical view of human anatomy, including an energetic physiology, as well as means to manage these resources; they embody more than philosophy.

Humans are assisted in taking their next steps by a blend of material and cognitive technologies. Bioenergetic technology is an example of this, as it reflects technological development based on a growing collective consciousness about energetic anatomy. Toltecs speed up their evolution by skilled use of imagination. As an aspect of their cognitive technology, the higher levels of imagination enable various time-travel modes of experience illustrated by out-of-body and near-death experiences.

Toltec abilities are derived, says don Juan, from *silent knowledge,* from awareness that is deep within us, perhaps at our very core, but outside the domain of reason.[45] Silent knowledge is a comprehensive knowing, a sense of natural order, a connection with infinity. Like other stable perceptions, it is a focal point position. Don Juan adds that years upon years ago, this was the natural condition of being human: that of behaving from silent knowledge. Then something occurred that created the ability to reason, and from that point we entered an evolutionary track concerned with objectifying our environment. The sense of being separate from the world created the beginnings of objectivity and vice versa. This new relationship with the world magnified the perception of living in a material world.

Both material and cognitive applications of awareness are needed for humans to grow, both are created from group consensus, and both need ethical tempering for effective use. Material technology is evolving so rapidly that its growth outpaces ethical considerations of how to use it. We have the means to quickly and completely destroy the inhabitability of our planet through warfare. For another example, manufacturing generally has not adjusted to the pollution it causes. For reasons such as this, His Holiness the Dalai Lama argues that religion remains relevant in modern society.[46] And religion scholar Paul Johnson notes, "Religious behavior seeks the largest possible adjustment of life, for it is concerned about the ultimate relationships."[47]

By locking perception within a box reflecting its own abilities, technology may estrange the individual from recognizing native abilities. It may also continue to grow at such a rate as to create more environmental destruction than benefit. And it may render futile the attempt to liberate a person or society from its grip. For his own field of bioethics, Leon R. Kass, author of *Life, Liberty and the Defense of Dignity,* argues for a more thorough examination of the discipline to develop a richer ethic.[48] Bioethics has grown from examinations of issues relating to death and dying while in a coma, to a range of topics such as transplants, stem cell research, and more.

Acknowledged as one of the founders of bioethics, Professor James Drane argues in *More Humane Medicine* that the doctor-patient relationship has changed. Patients have different assumptions relating to physician authority and treatment has become fragmented. Free-market capitalism now has a major influence on the relationship. Drane points out that these and other factors require a return to the traditional foundations of medical ethics to restore the personal bond between the physician and the person who is ill.[49]

Perhaps the growth of bioenergetics and transpersonal psychology will help produce an ethic for the development of consciousness. And maybe we need a technology and ethic that allows us to sufficiently command reason in such a manner as to cultivate silent knowledge. We would then have the power of a logically created system that paradoxically generates awareness through silent knowledge. This, in turn, would develop reason to make sense of an ever-expanding order—stimulation that would enhance the quality of life for one and all.

Education

As a species, we need to take better care of educational systems and methods. Perhaps the lack of relevance of what is being taught is affecting the secondary school dropout rate. And the entire ethic of curriculum needs to be overhauled. Gearing the education of children toward helping a country compete globally may diminish creativity in such a way as to produce the very opposite result. It may not only interfere with self-actualization but also may channel learning into predetermined categories often blocking new insights and therefore blocking the ability to develop technologies, the very qualities needed for success.

As reference, style of learning takes into account ontological factors such as responsibility, innate drives and pace, and emotional intelligence. Most important, it creates a solid and lasting relationship with learning. Initially developed by Benjamin Bloom, it is called "Mastery Learning"[50] and emphasizes consolidating a step in learning a skill or subject before moving on to the next step, and that creating an appropriate environment for this is essential. It is not rote learning, it is mastering the process of learning.

Teachers, administrators, and institutions exert tremendous entrainment influences on how we view our world. The quality of instruction makes all the difference in what is learned and how one relates to learning. This makes it all the more important for each person to assume responsibility for what is being learned and what to do about it. This allows one to offset poor instruction, if such is the case, and regain an edge for learning. Good instruction instills this attitude of personal responsibility. Excellent teaching requires it.

CREATING YOUR LIFE BY LIVING A PATH WITH HEART

Now we get to the heart of building a quality life. In Toltec, Buddhist, and other traditions this has come to be known as "living a path with heart." To fully engage life with abundant meaning, Jack Kornfield offers a range of perspectives and practices relating to inner transformation. Throughout his book, *A Path with Heart,* he provides perspectives on individual and group dynamics of growth. For instance, he deals with self-knowledge, expanding awareness, altered states, ethics, and applying meditation to psychotherapy.[51]

Don Juan boiled down the process of creating a path with heart to using your death as a way to focus your selection of involvements in life. The trick is to consult death in such a way that it doesn't become encumbering, to use death as a tool to battle fear rather than a morbid fixation. When making a decision, for example, make it in the light that it may well be your last act on Earth. Doing so helps bring to light the deepest drives and core values of a person.[52]

When you are suitably focused, the criteria for selecting the elements of your path are based on peace, strength, and joy. Once several pursuits have been initiated, you are on your path.[53] Rather than pursue money as a primary objective even though you really don't like the chase, you actively involve yourself with something else. Seen in the context of an energetic logic and ethic, having a large bank account is not errant, but going after money when it doesn't resonate with your core stultifies your growth. After several years of grooming your life based on peace, joy, and strength, you will have a life with that foundation.

Other teachers suggest similar approaches to finding, expressing, and living core meaning. To penetrate the shrouds of awareness that interfere with developing a full and complete life, meditation and healing-technique teacher Stephen Levine also advises us to use death as a focus to bring ourselves to life. He advocates that this helps us live in such a way as to "directly experience the moment-to-moment process that is our lives." And he also holds that it is fear (a condition characteristic of the orientation stage) that is the major impediment to this awareness.[54]

A leader of the positive psychology movement, Paul Pearsall points out the conditions of thriving include living a strong life, a deliberate life. As such he notes that peace and joy are aspects of such flourishing. Like others, he advises, "Don't die until you've lived."[55] Perhaps reflecting increased investigations into metaphysics, positive psychology shares common denominators with classic mysticism traditions. Both find that awareness and flourishing go hand in hand. They both aptly highlight the common focus relating to personal and group development.

People typically derive meaning in their lives from group values rather than from within. Jung tells us that this makes individuation impossible, as the self is never developed, let alone expressed and lived. For individual imagination to become alive and functional, we need to be able to step away from the group. At the same time we are social creatures who derive value from participation with the group. The balance is to seek individuation while keeping an eye on what you can offer others. In this way, you learn to be yourself while being part of the group, which is a measure of self-actualization.

Both personally and collectively, peace, joy, and strength characterize heightened consciousness. When these qualities are manifested, the components of a path with heart—the activities you decided to pursue—provide the means to solidify other gains. A life formed in such a way will help you reintegrate your awareness after you've stepped into an altered state.

Whether or not you cultivate OBEs or other *psi* experiences, ontological growth automatically produces altered states of consciousness by the simple fact of stretching into the unconscious, the unknown. How a person experiences this extension is often determined by training. A Toltec may have an OBE to better experience infinity while a Zen practitioner becomes more aware of infinity within a single breath. Organizing and implementing expanded awareness within a Toltec, Zen, or other psychological path is the same, though, as it is part of the trajectory of gradually becoming more aware en route to creating a new baseline state of consciousness. The elements of such creative paths provide a practical means for stability along the way.

Creating a path with heart is a way to begin working with cohesion.

It balances the forces inside and out. This produces more awareness as your life awakens your core. Remember, all of the influences throughout your life shape cohesion, the determinant of your perceptions and behaviors. Living a path with heart is a means to purposefully condition your energy body. This ongoing development is therefore a solid step toward *being*, a state that Levine describes as directly experiencing that "moment-to-moment process that is our lives."

8

The Unfolding Moment

Being, the capstone of ontological development, is a precise state of consciousness where creativity emanates from each and every instant. *Being* supersedes all models about it: whether the model is quantum physics or metaphysical cosmology, it falls to the wayside when you are actually in the moment. *Being* is a point from which you access infinity.

BEING

In *Being and Time,* Martin Heidegger offers three basic suppositions needed to study *being.* First, citing philosophical inquiry from Plato to Aristotle to Hegel, Heidegger regards *being* as the "most universal" concept and yet through centuries of investigation it has hardly been understood. Second, by nature it cannot be defined but this doesn't negate its meaning. Third, the quality of existence is self-evident. In each and every act, we use some aspect of *being.*[1]

Furthermore, he considers *being* as a "unitary phenomenon" and states that to study it we must define an ontological world that includes "being-in-the-world." With this grounding, Heidegger then declares that the new significant relationship of *being* enables us to transcend the worldly nature of life.[2] Yet he outlines *being* as consisting of oneness and the necessity to understand this from the point of view of daily life. Only then can we transcend this baseline state.

First published in 1927, *Being and Time* is firmly rooted in the Western European philosophical tradition. Although we may not be any better off today in understanding something so paradoxical and so intrinsic to the human experience, over the last fifty years a growing awareness about various forms of mysticism (of which *being* is an essential component), the work of psychologists such as Jung and Maslow (which pertains to fulfilling daily social needs to grow toward actualization), and now the advent of quantum physics (which reveals the intrinsic oneness of the universe), the nature of this little understood phenomenon is getting a closer look.

Within the scope of this work, *being* consists of maintaining a natural vibration, an ebb and flow between self and world, a grand harmony of energies within and without. In this exquisite state, you have a greater sense of self, a lightness of emotion, and a calm clarity that fills you with meaning. There is also a sense of oneness with all creation, and a feeling of having a personal place in the world. Paradoxically, this rhythm automatically carries with it the experience of nonattachment. As a result, the cosmos becomes impersonal.

Being is living in the moment, and the moment at hand is the crossroads for potential and actualization. The moment is where life is. Getting there and then staying there requires serious and disciplined effort, as *being* is perhaps the most sophisticated of all human behaviors.

Heightened Consciousness

Being may also be characterized as a constant state of heightened consciousness. It is the synthesis of learning and imagination, which produces a condition of artful living. In it, your first and second energy fields are communicating and working together to give you a full-body sense of living. This is your principal posture and orientation to navigate infinity.

The practice of heightened awareness takes you to possibility, to being able to handle a variety of focal point positions. You are now in a continually expanding world of new options, perceptions, and abilities. As you travel deeper to core the intensity of your experience increases; peak experiences, *psi*, and mystical experiences automatically result.

Maslow has mapped out *B-cognition*—*being*-related cognition—in detail, assigning characteristics and values to a range of behaviors such as problem solving, creativity, and peak experiences (whereas he sees *D-cognition* as being related to deficit needs). Some of the traits of B-cognition are total attention, richer perceptions, an altered state of time and space, and positive experience. The related values include a sense of oneness, fairness, beauty, simplicity, and autonomy.[3] B-cognition is an orientation toward self-actualization and the wellspring of creativity in all spheres of life.

While the wide-open awareness of B-cognition often supports deautomatization behaviors, Maslow also portrays it as having inherent dangers such as lack of action, diminishing personal responsibility, and too much tolerance.[4] It therefore needs to be attenuated so that practical daily requirements such as livelihood may be attended to. Adjusting for the downside of B-cognition is where solid metaphysics can add immeasurably. This augmentation of B-cognition then becomes a new class of behavior, which is the thrust of this book in that it contains an overview of the elements, goals, and results of a coherent, cognitive technology that impacts every aspect of our lives. We can call this behavior—the process of sustained and purposeful awareness of the moment—*M-cognition, moment*-related cognition. It is a creative endeavor in which we realize what has already been created inside us.

Core

Being arises from having a firm connection with your core. Typically, personality—the manner in which you express yourself—is formed in the light of social considerations. You make your way through life trying to meet your social needs by aligning with group consensus. This has certain beneficial results, yet doing so also estranges you from your individuality and so from your core. *Being* and M-cognition strategies and skills are not well understood, so how can they be cultivated en masse?

Usually personality is a facade. It is superficial. However, strategies like cultivating a path with heart provide a means to match personality with core. When you behave from your core, or at least orient yourself to core, your personality then matches the deepest regions of yourself. As a result, you are nurturing a natural energy field.

Ontological Intelligence

Just to make a point, let's say that a person who is truly *being* is at the genius level of ontological intelligence. This necessitates orchestrating and harmonizing all aspects of the self. Each chakra needs to be awakened and in resonance with the others. Personality and core need to match. Individual and social requirements need to be in harmony. This is quite an accomplishment.

The awakening of this form of intelligence places you in the new significant relationship Heidegger speaks of. How you make sense of the world and how you continue to behave intelligently is an entirely new class of behavior aching for full examination. Perhaps study of the mystical experience is a guiding light. Ontology is not just the study of the ways and means, the bits and pieces; it pertains to the whole of the person as measured by *being*. It also requires examination of all connections with the environment—the "being-in-the-world"—and all other behaviors involved with this "genius" level of living.

ELEMENTS OF BEING

Keeping in mind Heidegger's assertion that *being* is a whole and must be understood as such, here are aspects of that whole:

1. You experience a sense of eternity within the present moment. All time seems to emanate and expand from the present. You

can also relate to time in different ways, such as linear, nonlinear, or simultaneous. This flexibility in perceiving time diminishes when the main focus of attention is not on the present.

2. Hand in hand with this sense of eternity is the sense that you want to pay immediate attention to whatever is occurring. You are in the midst of eternity so the present is just as good a place to be as any other.

3. There is always the perception of newness. No matter how many times you travel along a certain route, there is always an impression that this is the first time you've passed that way.

4. You feel peaceful, relaxed. You might also feel a sense of well-being, from calm joy to ecstatic bliss.

5. You place the bulk of your attention on the environment and less on yourself. As you walk down a road, you pay more attention to the street, trees, people, what is happening in general, and less on your problems, concerns, joys, and other personal deliberations.

6. You feel a sense of rightness, of appropriateness. Everything in the universe is right and proceeding just fine. This might also be thought of as unconditional love.

7. You think less and use other faculties of perception such as feeling more. Thought removes us from experience (even the experience of thinking). The more we think and cultivate symbolic meaning, the more we extract our awareness from the essence of our lives. Putting an experience into words is not the experience; words represent the experience. Reason and thinking definitely have value for developing certain kinds of knowledge, but they can limit us to the "personality" of reality and keep us from direct experience.

8. You feel more in touch with your core.

9. You feel confident. Your perception has a good, clean edge that enhances clarity.

10. You recognize that any reality you perceive is a reflection of your-

self. You know that the way you relate to the world stems from the way you have trained your perception.

11. You have an innate sense of purpose. You feel meaning in your life.

12. You feel nonattached. You strive to do your best, but you are not tied to the results of your actions.

13. You feel balanced. Your physical and nonphysical energies work in harmony without the need to labor for balance.

14. You *are* and so you have less a need to know. In other words, you know you don't know what the world truly is, and that is just fine. You are comfortable with the mystery of infinity . . . so fundamentalism doesn't take root.

15. You are aware of multilevels of experience occurring simultaneously. The more you learn about a given procedure, the more likely you are to apply that knowledge. The more you apply knowledge, the more you will innovate, or arrive at new applications. While in a state of *being,* learning, application, and innovation occur automatically. You generate creative solutions without the usual effort expended on this kind of task. These levels of experience work automatically as part of a natural, spontaneous order within your life.

This list could go on and on. But even trying to describe *being* by listing attributes may be somewhat foolhardy, because it is a state of consciousness beyond description. If you are in it, overanalysis will almost surely take you back out of it. But by knowing what to look for, you can begin to align your perception in the direction of this experience. In a nutshell, *being* consists of a continual, direct connection between self and world. It allows you to access the infinite within yourself.

BECOMING

Maslow maintains that self-actualization is everything that a person can become, an ultimate goal. But we can't see what we can become because we are dominated by whatever need is at hand.[5] So *becoming* is a constant venture into the unknown. It is the ability to move toward *being,* to move with life's experiences by saturating yourself in each moment and, at the same time, by completely letting go of each moment. It is an unfolding. The conditions of your life emanate from that instant. Viewed in this way, learning is *becoming* and vice versa. The manner of growth is *becoming.*

Maslow asserts, "*being* and *becoming* are not contradictory or mutually exclusive." Both are rewarding.[6] Both require simultaneously connecting with potential and allowing that connection to give rise to actuality. Maintaining *being* requires constant *becoming* and constant *becoming* takes you to *being.* Neither is static, closed, or dogmatic. The two arise from a continual dance with learning and imagination, with potential, and with infinity. In this dance you need to entertain the possibilities and move toward those that resonate with core. But if you identify too much with these goals, you will once again pin perception to the definition, to the thoughts, rather than to the experience. That will prevent you from awakening completely, from the actual energy of the venture. You will then succumb to closure, which blocks *becoming.*

As you awaken your energy body, you automatically activate latent capacities of perception such as the cornerstones. Developing these gives rise to factors that are similar to those found in the dynamic of *becoming* and *being.* Don Juan says that *seeing* is the greatest accomplishment of an artisan because *seeing* places you at the doorstep of mastery. Yet a person can lose him- or herself in the intricacies of what is being *seen.* As a result, the person becomes less objective and more obsessed, thereby ending the more robust ontological development of the energy body. The immediate consequence is that the person fixates the focal point rather than coming to terms with its relativity. This is a key point, he says, in understanding the inherent properties of perception.[7]

The idea is to remain unbiased to allow *seeing* to reveal more and more of what humans and the world are. This only occurs through *becoming.* It is the descriptions of reality that ensnarl us, states don

Juan. If we remain unbiased and free as we learn, we stand a chance of complete awakening.[8]

Physicist Roger Jones helps place this in another context. He notes that Newtonian science contended that there is a clearly defined, objective world that exists independently of observation. With the advent of quantum physics, the role of the observer came into consideration, as did the notion that what is being observed can't be separated from the observer; that is, by the very nature of quantum theory the observer and that which is being observed are entangled.[9] The consciousness of the observer, then, directly influences what is being observed. The point here is that when measured against infinity there is no accounting for what is perceived, no encapsulating it. A new model, as measured by a new focal point position, will always emerge, as we get better at perceiving infinity.

Flow

A main characteristic of *being* is *flow* and *flow* aptly characterizes *becoming*. The notion of *flow* is explored by psychologist Mihaly Csikszentmihalyi in *Flow: The Psychology of Optimal Experience*. Csikszentmihalyi says that joy, creativity, and total involvement with life are all aspects of *flow*, and are all conditions of optimal experience.[10] Furthermore, Daniel Goleman says that being able to enter *flow* is "emotional intelligence at its best; *flow* [italics mine] represents perhaps the ultimate in harnessing the emotions in the service of performance and learning."[11]

Accordingly, entering *flow* is not a haphazard, far-fetched proposition. It is simply a challenge to jettison everything that holds you back, and then catapult your awareness into regions that remain unimaginable for most. *Flow* occurs as a result of adeptly navigating potential. A certain degree of abandon is necessary to cultivate it. You have to push forward. Relaxation is also needed. Even in strenuous athletic activity, relaxation is a main ingredient for optimal performance.[12] Relaxation is also essential to develop a natural energy field. A natural energy field has no ordinary definition, so you don't have to maintain it by force. Residing in a natural field maintains *flow*. And this works hand in hand with heightened consciousness.

Timing

As Heidegger maintains, time offers the possibility of moving forward, of *becoming*.[13] *Being* is residing in the continuously unfolding moment and for this timing is essential. Timing in this sense means you have keen awareness of your place in the world and how to effectively navigate your path through daily life. An unnatural pace blocks imagination and learning, and thus *becoming,* so you need to discover your natural pace in all activities. Cultivating emotional intelligence is a strong step forward in learning innate timing. This refined balance with the world automatically leads to peak experiences. Timing, then, stems from awareness of the moment, allows you to connect directly with the world, and promotes quality of life.

Another effect of developing timing is that you experience a shift from reviewing time to looking into the face of time, a characteristic of *being*. Usually, we view time as linear, aligning our perception so that we view time as occurring from the past to the present to the future. To make a decision, we call upon past experiences and project that information into the future, thinking the stability of the future is held together by events of the past. We see continuity in another's behavior based on our experiences with them and then get disgruntled if their behavior doesn't fit our expectations. As we create the order of our world based on a linear progression of time, it becomes a major force affecting our perception. We forget it is a convenient arrangement to help us make sense of our experiences and lose ourselves thinking it is the only way the world works.

To face time, you must maneuver your cohesion to a new position. You must face upriver, so to speak, to witness the origins of linear time. This has the simultaneous effect of enabling you to hook onto potential, to nonlinear time that spreads in many directions. This helps generate *flow*. However, time and *flow* may be viewed as entirely separate dynamics. *Flow* is related to achieving a solid alignment with an emanation and then feeling the resulting resonance of energies, whereas time and timing are the measurement of this action.

To have proper timing, you must gain masterful control of your energy body, which involves a highly refined balance with the world. Hence, proficiency with timing rests in the artisan stage.[14] As an artisan, you can step away from the familiar and bring potential into play through *becoming-being*. To make a good go of it, your instincts must be sharp. You must be able to sense how to behave in the given moment and from this awareness have your livelihood provided for, at the same time as the groundwork for what will be needed in the future is automatically laid. To derive concrete value from *being*, it must facilitate and augment survival. This is where M-cognition deserves further research and illumination.

Timing allows cohesion to make necessary adjustments naturally and thereby helps you remain aware of core. As a result, more of the energy body awakens. Thinking then reflects *becoming* rather than functioning as mechanical and static projection-reflection. Feeling turns into a measurement for timing, enhancing emotional intelligence. Valerie Hunt's "mind field organizer" of emotions then produces new cohesions. In the Toltec framework, we can understand "mind" as being synonymous with energy body and cohesion as the "organization" of the mind. Completing the loop, thinking then *flows*, or *becomes*, from this emotion-based organization of perception. This entire endeavor brings about awareness of *will*, the epicenter of the cornerstones and the ballast for the entire energy body.

WILL AND INTENT

If we really can't talk about *being*, then why is there all this talk? First, it is the nature of humans to reflect and project, to examine their conditions and figure out the possibilities. Also related to the task at hand, modern Toltecs have learned to reason their way out of reason. Part of their emerging style is to make leaving reason in service of developing the whole of the organism an entirely reasonable proposition, in which reason gradually gives way to *will*. This is the proverbial slippery slope, as reason also likes to have its way, as it were, and so fixates attention. Closure and fundamentalism are often the effects of well-crafted rational arguments. Like other aspects of ontological growth, the balance between reason and *will* requires deft skill. The only true way to learn any ontological skill is to actively engage it. Discover for yourself what it takes to bring you to life.

Will is the governing force of cohesion and a determinant of the location of the focal point.[15] To awaken *will,* you have to step outside of your thoughts . . . all of them. At the same time, you must tap capacities of yourself that provide all of the sense that thinking provides, plus more. You can't cut off your thoughts and hope everything will come out just fine. If you arbitrarily leave thinking behind without another form of guidance, you will be rudderless in a stormy sea. The stages of growth act as channel markers to allow you to gradually, steadily, and surely form a new relation with the world. To load the chances in favor of success, your venture must be done consciously, not randomly.

Will is the basic energetic force that moves cohesion to allow new perceptions. *Will* always performs this function; for most, it remains latent, doing its work without conscious awareness, which results in a diminution of potential. In the Toltec model, sustained *being* presupposes having activated *will* and having done so while being oriented toward a natural field. It is quite possible to activate *will* but remain in the craftsmanship stage as *will* permits you to create myriad conditional energy fields, many of which might actually prevent further growth.

A permanent baseline shift toward *will* occurs when you place the accent of your daily life on imagination and feeling. Rather than go through the day referencing what you have learned, or are learning, you sense the fuller energies of the world by giving precedence to your emotional intelligence and your sense of imagination. From this posture, you allow learning and thinking to come and go like the ebb and flow of the tides. As a result, your life takes on a dreamlike quality. You stay focused and grounded, though, by your intent.

Intent is the active and deliberate focusing of *will*.[16] *Becoming* is developed through consciously applying intent for that result. Intention doesn't exist solely for this purpose, though. It is a natural ability affecting all spheres of life that is beginning to receive rigorous examination. As mentioned in chapter one, intent is under scientific scrutiny as a determinant in remote healing.

Csikszentmihalyi says that consciousness is "intentionally ordered information."[17] "Order" includes all kinds of organization, not just verbal information. It arises from a stable cohesion. This type of awareness exists as a result of thinking as well as anything that enhances cognition in general. It is also the natural world. Oceans contain order, as do jungles. How humans perceive that order is another matter. To supplant the order of an ordinary cohesion for that of *being* requires extended effort.

Csikszentmihalyi also says that intention is the force that maintains order.[18] And so we have the stable intent of *being* and the intent of movement and growth found in *becoming*. By relaxing into this pair, and by remaining vigilant to the work, you bring both to life. You *become* conscious. In so doing, you bring yourself to life in a most remarkable and intelligent manner. If you have the ability to manage your life, to generate positive experiences, to keep growing in leaps and bounds, and all the while have your awareness flooded with life each and every moment, then you are an intelligent human being.

Will generates possibility. Managing this is where intent comes in. It keeps cohesion together, keeps awareness ordered, and maintains your life. It also allows you to access new order, new cohesions. By the time you get to a natural field, you are well beyond ordinary meaning. For, as don Juan says, his *will* is what keeps him alive regardless of his personal choice, or regardless of anything he thinks or *sees* about the world.[19] Having stepped into imagination to that degree, he has become a living part of the magic of all creation.

NAVIGATING INFINITY

The stages of personal evolution are steps to awaken the energy body. *Being* is an effect, a derivative of long and arduous work to bring yourself to life. As you travel through the stages, the active ingredient of *being* is found in *becoming*, which is the motion of creativity. Arriving at *being* requires having a precise life.

In the film *Apollo 13* astronauts returning from the moon had a disabled spacecraft. Based on the true story of NASA's Apollo 13 trek into space, the film depicts oxygen tanks rupturing, electrical systems failing, and the astronauts truly put to the test. To reenter Earth's atmosphere safely, they had to navigate their craft within a paper-thin margin. If they had failed they would have bounced off Earth's atmosphere like a billiard ball, to be sent speeding through space to meet their certain doom. Likewise, sailing the seas of infinity requires navigating a razor-thin margin. The odds are staggering, but don Juan and others have hit the mark. Why not you?

To do this, you need to be in *flow*. To stay in *flow*, you have to let go. When you let go, you open yourself to many different influences. Timing plays a critical role in helping you stay focused, and not being random about your life. You must retain purpose of mind and manner. You need to have your bearings. This is where guidance comes in; for that there are a variety of navigational tools.

Cognition

Typically, cognitive guidance pertains to the mental influences that govern our behavior. In *Emotional Intelligence,* Goleman makes the point that uncontrolled anger results from a lack of cognitive guidance. He says it's an inability to control base-level emotions through the application of reason. He also indicates that many of our emotional memories that have evolved over thousands of years may be out of date, "especially in the fluid social world we humans inhabit."[20] If so, these emotional guideposts produce behaviors that haven't kept pace with the world we've built. As a result, we are out of touch. We are out of balance. And our timing is certainly off.

Thought focuses energy. In fact, Goleman points out that thought is a major influence in determining which emotions are experienced.[21] In addition, thought is so powerful it produces entire worldviews, entire realities. But, again, these are only intellectual constructions. The meaning of cognitive guidance needs to be stretched out to cover any mode of perception that promotes awareness, understanding, and knowledge. As emotions organize perception, they need to be understood as a part of cognition, along with the other cornerstones, chakras, and anything else that increases consciousness and learning. Cognition is therefore intimately intertwined with ontological intelligence, the full scope of awareness.

Metaphysical systems are cognitive technologies. A philosophy contains a worldview and techniques that bring the worldview to life. The system can help you learn *becoming,* which then allows your thoughts and feelings to enter more expansive orders of awareness. But a metaphysical guidance system that accounts for so much can be quite intimidating. In fact, a good system can account for anything you experience. The problem is that you might lose yourself in the gyroscope and not sail the ocean in front of you. To avoid this danger, a good guidance system teaches you self-guidance, not dogma. A viable system portrays its teachings as a form of guidance, not as a completely accurate picture of reality. As a result, when you aim your intent, the guidance it provides keeps you on track. You then develop your own guidance system. You learn how to think, feel, and *see* for yourself, which transforms outer guidance into inner guidance. When you learn this, you are on your way to activating *will,* which delivers an even more powerful form of guidance. In terms of cognition, you are substantially more aware.

Instinct and Intuition

Another form of guidance is provided by the often-subtle perceptions of instinct and intuition. The difference between them is that instinct pertains to "any natural and apparently innate drive or motivation," whereas intuition is "immediate understanding, knowledge, or awareness derived neither from perception nor reasoning."[22] Instinct is often considered a more biologic response and intuition related to general awareness. Both result from a direct connection with the environment. In each case, your capacity to respond makes all the difference.

In the best-selling book, *Blink,* Jerome Malcolm says that experience educates intuition and instinct.[23] There is no question that experience educates instinct, especially when instinct is often considered an effect of conditioned responses. But in the operation of intuition, it may be that experience allows the person to accept the awareness, that is, the person permits the information to become conscious based on having an established relation with it.

Behaving in new ways makes the energy body glow, says don Juan.[24] In other words, experience expands the conscious field. A scientific correlate is that behavior and experience affect neural pathways.[25] With an increase of types or repetitions of behaviors or experiences, more of the brain is activated. Such correlations between brain functions and cohesion make brain physiology a useful reference for the study of the energy body and vice versa.

Healer Carolyn Myss uses intuition to diagnose physical disorders. Her skills stretch to being able to do so nonlocally; that is, with great physical distance separating her and the subject.[26] And Einstein found that there is no logical path to the elementary laws of physics, so arriving at them was a function of intuition.[27] Don Juan maintains that intuition is totally accurate unless the information is clouded by personal considerations.[28] This assertion is backed by psychological research demonstrating that intuition can be highly accurate, but prejudice and fear can lead one in the wrong direction.[29]

The subtlety of instinct and intuition can make it seem that one who is *being* doesn't think, at least in ordinary terms. Well-developed intuition reflects a marked degree of proficiency with silent knowledge; this type of relation with the world turns learning into art.

Experts

Whether you need new plumbing or a surgical operation, there is no doubt that advice from experts may save the day. Expert guidance is especially valuable when you either cannot discern your way clearly or you actively follow poor inner guidance. Within the stockroom of mirrors, there are plenty of false images and echoes. Often these distortions result from excessive personal desire, unethical power plays, fear, or worry. External reference points can offer good feedback to enable you to test and measure inner guidance. An expert may help you to orient yourself, or at least provide a sounding board so you can work through the problem. This kind of guidance can help you to break through the projective effects of conditional fields that shape your perception.

The other side of turning to experts is that we have a marked tendency to look outside of ourselves for answers, blindly follow authority, and relinquish personal responsibility: the epitome of dysfunctional guidance. To counteract this tendency and help you to stay true to your path, it is good to remember that, whatever their specialty, experts abide by their model. After all, that's where their expertise comes from. But there are times when experts know so much they have forgotten the basics. Lack of touch with the fundamentals may even lead to fundamentalism.

In his critically acclaimed book, *How Doctors Think,* physician Jerome Groopman explains that doctors may make incorrect diagnoses due to "attribution errors." That is, they base a diagnosis on stereotypes.[30] When a diagnosis stems from this form of projection, it may lead to the patient receiving the wrong treatment. Similarly, Shunryu Suzuki tells us, "In beginner's mind there are many possibilities; in expert's mind there are few."[31] The Zen student is encouraged to reclaim his or her "original mind," which relates to consciousness that is neither closed nor full. It is empty yet attentive. It is assured and peaceful. This Zen teacher sounds like Maslow describing B-cognition.

Environmental Indications

New weather patterns, melting glaciers, and disappearing species are examples of the world providing guidance. Guidance derived from environmental conditions of one sort or another has long been honored. In his landmark book, *The Origins of Consciousness in the Breakdown of the Bicameral Mind,* Julian Jaynes outlines several forms of guidance or divination.[32] From the arrangement of sticks on a floor to the swirl of oil, to various forms of omens, humans have always sought to make sense out of their world by looking directly at it, or rather *seeing* into it.

Moreover, Toltecs have developed a sophisticated manner of discerning omens by forming a language based on symbols that permits communication between oneself and the world.[33] Specific colors, for example, carry precise meaning. That meaning is conveyed when a certain color appears, especially if it does so in an out-of-the-ordinary manner. The way in which this type of communication has been formed is similar if not identical to the manner in which written, cultural languages are developed.

The siren of a police car provides guidance and, in a general fashion, so do the laws governing behavior. Certainly a road hazard sign is an environmental indication worth heeding. At the level of *being,* the necessities of personal navigation take on more delicate nuances. A natural field requires you to step beyond conditional fields to participate fully with the environment. Whatever occurs in your life is part of a pattern. The pattern may be unfolding or a remnant of that which is passing. The key is to pay attention. The means of navigation, from intuition to rules of the road, are then learned step by step as you progress along the ontological path.

Meditation and Prayer

Another form of guidance is found in meditation and prayer. It arises from listening to what bubbles forth from your consciousness, either from just being aware or by generating a question that, in a sonarlike manner, results in some form of revelation. Sometimes meditation and prayer are difficult to separate into discrete functions. Other times, they are driven by specific religious or psychological techniques. Psychologist Charles Tart refers to meditation as "practices intended to change the quality or state of consciousness of your mind." Prayer, he maintains, "is effective insofar as there is a 'supernatural' or nonordinary order of Being or beings who might respond to it."[34]

Meditation has been scientifically shown to affect emotions in a positive way and in some studies meditators reported a higher level of contentment than nonmediators.[35] Prayer, in turn, has been shown to promote healing, whether the patient is nearby or at a distance from the healer.[36] Both meditation and prayer use intent but in different ways. Meditative guidance is typically the more passive while prayer the more active. In both cases, the quality of guidance arises from how well one is focused on, or attentive to, the depths of infinity.

Path with Heart

With all the energies swirling about, you need focus to get on in the world. You need a rudder. This is where the path with heart plays a significant role. In the previous chapter, the guideline given for creating this path focused on participating in those areas of life that provide peace, joy, and strength. The objective is a life with meaning. In the more expansive pursuit of personal development, a path with heart plays other critical roles.

A path formed in this way also orients you to core, your natural intent. As a result, your life closes off in natural ways. You can't do everything, so the items you select automatically perform the learning function of closure and simultaneously remaining open. You augment your life rather than force it to conform to rules that don't match your sensibilities. The idea is to learn who you are and how to parlay that into a good life. The elements of your path—livelihood, family, profession, and so on—are not the real deal. *Living* your life is. A path with heart represents a way of navigating infinity that promotes such an endeavor.

This orientation also helps you find your personal timing, your individual relation with yourself, those about you, and the greater world. Your sense of connectedness with all areas of your life enhances your passion. In turn, timing enables you to sustain *being.* The circle of infinity forms yet again as *being* enhances your connectedness and so your path. The more you cultivate your path, the better your timing. By the time you reach the artisan stage, your timing demonstrates moment-to-moment precision.

Reflecting your growth, the elements of your path will change over time. Knowing that any path might end, or that you might step off a path at any moment, helps to center you in the moment and to prevent you from thinking about how your life should unfold. While you can't do everything, you can learn to *become* everything. You can then let your life unfold. Don Juan says that this results from proficient *seeing* and is marked by the capacity to seemingly vanish while remaining totally present.[37]

With pure learning, what you see today is different from what you observed yesterday or will tomorrow. The entire universe is *becoming,* and conditional fields blind us to that awareness. By orienting yourself to core, the circumstances of your life begin to occur naturally. You then find your own place in the world, and gracefully live the *being* and *becoming* of it.

Becoming-being contains the atmosphere of ongoing renewal, of continual discovery. It is a radical reformation of your baseline state of consciousness characterized by a natural field: awareness that has been there all along but is discovered only in the moment. It also reflects complete entrainment to your personal emanation. This enables you to consolidate your life, including setting the stage for the future while remaining steadfastly in the present. Managing your life so that you tune yourself to this requires developing the many facets of body knowledge.

Body Knowledge

In some way, shape, or form, all guidance hinges on body knowledge, learning all of your innate capacities such as those outlined throughout this book. As such, each navigational tool requires paying attention to what the body senses, and to how you relate to any given event. By using your entire body—your entire anatomy—you gain the ability to connect intimately with the world.

Full body knowledge is governed by *will* and directed by intent. Developing and maintaining *being* centers on body knowledge. It is a natural effect of continually awakening potential into realization, of staying in touch with infinity and allowing that connection to pull the best out of you. As a result, the cornerstones of perception are all functioning, and each mode of perception is joined into a unified whole, thereby making it possible for you to have a unique relation with the world. Your path with heart is an avenue to this level of realization. Your life will then evolve to something beyond your current imagination.

Consolidating all of these perspectives into a map that provides a greater understanding of human consciousness and the world we live in is the work at hand. A first step is that of gaining awareness that these options exist in the first place. Then coming to terms with their scope requires the development of the appropriate cognitive tools, abilities, and approaches. M-cognition—which essentially covers the muscle to mystical spectrum of mind—represents body knowledge at its finest, a utilization of an extended human anatomy. It also offers an initial reference by illuminating a solid orientation to *becoming-being*. That prepares us to embark on the grandest of adventures, a voyage into the unknown that is navigated by our connection with infinity.

Energy Management Skills

The following techniques and perspectives are universal. They apply to everyone regardless of the chosen path. They are intended to disrupt habitual responses, to rearrange how you look at the world, and to liberate perception. They are part of the technological gears that enable the management of cohesion.

Overall, these skills destabilize conditional fields in such a way as to enable the energy body to become more conscious. Many resources pertaining to these types of skills are readily available, including those referenced throughout this book.

DEAUTOMATIZATION

The essence of deautomatization is to allow dormant abilities to awaken by suspending the day-to-day consciousness of that which is known. The style and manner of an exercise is subordinate to the raw exertion coupled with the intent to fully engage a skill. It is what don Juan calls *not-doing*.[1]

Even though closure is necessary for learning, deautomatization prevents too much closure. A key to managing the deleterious effects of fundamentalism is to accept a teaching while simultaneously letting it go, to allow new relationships to emerge. For this, you need to add the ingredients of personal responsibility, independent thinking and feeling, nonattachment, fluidity, constantly challenging assumptions about reality, minimizing self-reflection, and utilizing everything else that a workable philosophy provides, including leaving the philosophy behind.

The core of deautomatization is to remain unbiased by interpretations including those arising from models of reality. In other words, you don't assume the implicit facts of reality, be they small or large in scope. "Reality" once held the world as flat, or subsequently that all pieces of the world are not connected. Copernicus and quantum physics, respectively, dissolved those views. It is a mistake to think that new worldviews won't emerge.

One significant advantage of this concept-free state is granting you the ability to break the boundaries of your normal way of viewing and interacting with the world. You can also reconcile opposites and so find balance in the midst of the push and pull of differing values and standards. You then have new options, behaviors, and problem-solving capacities. Maslow's B-cognition deals directly with this, including the inherent difficulties it presents as outlined in chapter eight.

Practicing feeling and developing emotional intelligence, which go hand in hand, are substantial means to reorient your stance in this world, a principal effect of deautomatization. One way to focus on feeling is to pay attention kinesthetically; that is, to discern the sensations in your muscles and physical body in general. The perspectives that follow are also in this category of managing consciousness.

Self-Reflection

Self-reflection results from internal dialogue. This is the incessant verbiage about the world being one way or another. It builds cohesion and may also lock your focal point into place.[2] What you think about the world may, or may not, be true. Whatever the case, it is a force to be reckoned with. Tart holds that our internal dialogue continually reinforces group consensus and "it absorbs such a large amount of our attention/awareness energy that we have little of that energy available for other processes."[3]

Stopping this internal chatter is a major way to step out of conditional fields. When you are taught to talk, says don Juan, you are taught to dull yourself.[4] The day-in and day-out references to the same things reduce the flow of energy between you and the environment. At the same time, he states that the more fluid and varied your internal dialogue is, the more resilient you are.[5] This is part of reasoning yourself out of reason into a more expanded participation with the world.

Furthermore, an artisan doesn't think.[6] The stockroom mirrors have been so well cleansed that there is no reflecting or projecting. There's only the immediacy of the moment to be lived, the *being* of it. It is by getting out of yourself, so to speak, that you cultivate heightened consciousness.

As an exercise, stopping self-reflection allows the environment—from the general conditions of your life to the greater cosmological expanse—to have greater influence. All deautomatization skills help you step outside your thoughts. Don Juan also prescribes a meditative walk for this as well.[7]

As an example of this procedure:

1. Walk with your hands in an unusual position that does not attract attention. The novelty directs energy away from the ordinary pattern of attention created by your usual way of walking. If you hold your hands in a dramatically unusual position, you have to contend with other people sending their energies toward you as they wonder what you're doing.

2. Direct your vision toward the horizon. If you are in a hill or mountain environment, look 10–40 feet in front of you. If you look 20 feet away, for instance, as you walk continue looking 20 feet away.

3. Unfocus your eyes, allowing your peripheral vision to absorb as much as possible.

4. Listen to and smell the environment. Feel your surroundings. You're trying to get out of your thoughts and into your body.

5. Walk at a normal pace, or slower than your normal pace.

6. For safety, walk where you don't have to contend with traffic or other obstacles. Otherwise, you're thinking about navigating rather than interrupting your thinking.

7. Once you gain competency with turning off your flow of thoughts, you can do so "simply" by intending it.

Entrainment and Resistance

To be conscious of how your cohesion forms, it is important to become aware of the basic maneuvers of opening up and closing off influences that shape you. By actively entraining your perception, such as forming a path with heart, you accept and flow with energy. With resistance, you block a condition or circumstance from taking root. As a result, you may completely step away from a seductive influence or resist it in such a way as to study it. You might examine personal and professional peer pressures in such a manner, for instance.

Blind refusal to acknowledge a circumstance is entrainment rather than resistance, as doing so keeps a conditional field locked in place and therefore entrainment to that field occurs automatically. Deautomatization is meant to suspend these types of behaviors. Faith in a divine order or being, on the other hand, is entraining to a higher level of participation with the world. Don Juan referred to this combination of being open and/or closed as being accessible or inaccessible and he encouraged accessibility to Spirit.[8] This means developing core awareness or living with the awareness of residing within infinity.

He also thought that worry entrained perception in a negative manner. When you lose your bearings and become too centered in what others think, you entrain to group consciousness rather than staying focused on self-actualization.[9] In this light, worry is succumbing rather than creating. This is neatly contrasted with constructive reflection where you might contemplate and consider rather than develop hard-and-fast interpretations, an activity Goleman finds helpful in cultivating emotional intelligence.[10]

The balance of these various perspectives is found in maintaining your own sense of self and consciously choosing that which you wish to align with. It requires personal responsibility and an orientation toward growth. It is the center point of how you connect with the world.

Balance

The more your cohesion shifts, the more your world becomes fluid, and will perhaps seem unstable from time to time during transitions between cohesions. Altered states, including spontaneous *psi,* mystical experiences, and all sorts of nonsensical things might happen. To deal with this, you must continually adjust and adapt. This is where balance comes in. It is like a combination of patience, awareness, perseverance, and fluidity—not to mention the timing involved in knowing where you want to go, what your priorities are, and what you aim to do along the way.

A core ingredient of balance is being grounded. This means you have your own life, your own solid sense of yourself. The path with heart addresses this. But it also means you are experiencing a complete flow of energy. Charles Tart advocates balanced development of the body, intellect, and emotions.[11] Each influences the others.

Release and Recharge

You can't develop new cohesion when holding on to the old. James Oschman references energetic representations or "signatures" of trauma and contends that they are resolvable.[12] In general, you need to refresh your energy body just as you would take a shower. In Toltec literature, a principal means to do this is through the *recapitulation.* The essence of this practice is to methodically review, release, and recharge all your energies. A variety of Toltec sources outline procedures for loosening the energetic bindings that hold perception static.[13]

Tart says that prayer is recapitulation, as you remind yourself of your knowledge and intention; its effectiveness hinges on the amount of consciousness brought to the exercise.[14] And you can't beat plain and simple laughter to help you release and recharge.

By paying attention to the breath, it is often the initial reference point for the recapitulation. In many metaphysical traditions breath work is integral. In Zen it is the doorway that connects inner and outer and acts as a centering point for meditation.[15] When proficiency in recapitulation has been developed, it is possible to eliminate this step and directly apply intent to accomplish results. There is also a variety of other energy cleansing techniques. Reiki teachings, for example, acknowledge the habitual patterns that are unconsciously maintained and the need to resolve these emotional patterns.[16]

The essential ingredient of these approaches is allowing core energy to surface. Recapitulation exercises allow you to let go of cohesion automatically, so you may then let go of worry, discomfort, and that argument you just had. *Becoming* is also a state of letting go that requires letting go of good things in life as well. You don't turn your back on them; you let go of the moment that contained them. A path with heart sets the stage to allow "good" moments to keep occurring.

A shamanic variation of the recapitulation is:

1. Place your chin near your right shoulder. Now move it in a smooth, sweeping motion to your left shoulder. Then back to your right shoulder.
2. As you repeat step 1, inhale through your nose as you sweep from right to left, and exhale through your mouth as you sweep from left to right.
3. To warm up, perform the first sweep (right to left) as you inhale, and then return your head to a relaxed position looking straight ahead as you exhale. Henceforth, perform both sweeps as indicated in steps 1 and 2.

4. Now as you breathe in, intend your breath to pull in the energy of the event, person, or feeling you're working with. Feel yourself connect with your subject of study, then use your breath to bring that energy into your body. To get a sense of this, pick a minor event that is still somewhat troubling to you.

5. As you tap your memories, work from the items surrounding the event, to the people involved, to your feelings.

6. Let your body do the work. Your part is to engage the exercise and, above all, *intend* the recapitulation to occur.

7. Immerse yourself in your memories without indulging. Allow yourself to fully relive the occurrence.

8. Now it's time to yield to the energy. Let it work within you so you enter all the crevices you have forgotten.

9. Allow the energy to dissipate of its own accord. This facilitates realigning your energy fields.

10. Get in the habit of reviewing and releasing anywhere, anytime. Even in the middle of a business conference, you can unobtrusively make one or two breathing sweeps and release energy that spontaneously surfaced. You also find that your intent sets the recapitulation process in motion whether or not you perform the breathing sweeps. What matters most is intending the recapitulation, not the specific manner of doing so. As a result, you may feel energy moving and releasing anytime, anywhere.

Relaxation

After dismissing the positive claims of meditators, physician Herbert Benson eventually decided to at least take a look. He then clinically observed "striking physiologic changes" in meditators that included lowered heart rate, metabolic rate, and breathing rate.[17] The connections between relaxation produced by meditation and good health were obvious and Benson went on to write his best-selling book, *The Relaxation Response,* which has remained an important work for over thirty years.

Tart points out that relaxation promotes meditation and meditation enhances relaxation.[18] He goes on to say, conversely, that one set of psychological structures may prevent another from functioning. Relaxation could help a person minimize physical pain but the pain might be too overwhelming to allow relaxation.[19] Cohesion is a psychological structure. With a disorder such as pain, relaxation might interfere with how cohesion binds and so the coherence of "pain" is removed. But if the pain were too overwhelming to permit this, then perhaps the combination of a recapitulation exercise and relaxation would be successful. The recapitulation could lessen the coherence of the "pain" cohesion, then relaxation could step in to allow the resolution of tension, thereby minimizing or removing the pain.

While relaxation may not always be effective by itself, energy psychologist Gallo backs up the general principle by indicating that when trying to remove trauma, relaxation lessens anxiety and encourages healing.[20] Relaxation, then, allows energy to shift and new awareness to surface. It makes you generally more competent.

Decisions

A decision reflects the consolidation of cohesion. Not wavering from a decision is a means to build cohesion. Unchangeable decisions, says don Juan, groom unbending intent.[21] He advocates not changing a decision unless it is by another decision. In other words, he removes equivocation. He also advises us to make decisions free from fear or ambition.[22] In short, he uses character to build the energy body's resources. Whether decisions are based on deficit or growth needs, or whether or not free will exists, the basis for decision-making is awareness and responsibility. He also doesn't look back, which promotes *becoming*.

Nonattachment

Nonattachment is an investigative tool; it is not severance from anything. It is a way to understand life, maintains Suzuki. It is when emphasis is placed on particular points that difficulties with attachment arise.[23]

Tart says that nonattachment is "learning to 'look neutrally' on *whatever* happens, learning to pay full attention to stimuli and reactions but not to identify with them." He adds that while nonattachment helps the machinery of the mind run better, there may be difficulties. One is that when a person seems unaffected he or she might really be uptight. The other problem occurs when new situations occur and the person has had no practice with them and so acts inappropriately.[24]

Nonattachment also augments *becoming,* as you need to feel and think freely. Don Juan says that a person who is nonattached has only one thing: the power of decisions. When this is added to awareness of death, he continues, it provides for a life of efficiency and gusto.[25] In turn, the thing to do when you act inappropriately is to not fret and to regain your nonattachment. As a result, you are engaging deautomatization.

Habituation

Self-reflection is typically *habituated* thinking, in which awareness remains focused on the same options and repetition cements a number of elements in place. You need the routine of habits to form cohesion. This works positively such as in all the habits you perform to be professional at work. At the same time, habits lock perception in place.

To say this another way, neurologist Donald Calne cites habituation as the oldest form of learning.[26] Repetition is a primary education tool. But to add to the skill of learning and to form new cohesions, you must be able to hold what is known in abeyance to determine its value.

The way to do this is to alter your routines. This could be as simple as reversing the way you put on your belt, or what time you have lunch. What is needed is disrupting influences that shake up cohesion. Remember, new behaviors stimulate both the energy body and neural pathways.

In general, deautomatization is rearranging habits already developed, forming new habits for new behaviors, letting go of expectations of results, and practicing new modes of perception. Dishabituation—

altering the routines that bind cohesion and forge neural pathways—is an antidote to fundamentalism. Otherwise, your life becomes a stereotype rather than the vital force it should be.

Self-Observation

The mystic Gurdjieff thought that "seeing oneself" was an important part of self-remembering, remembering all the things that are a part of you, even if not yet recognized. It is therefore a catalyst for self-knowledge, and yet it doesn't mean you will really know yourself.[27] Not knowing yourself can be a good thing in that you continually allow new facets of yourself to surface.

Context—what you think applies to a situation—facilitates self-observation. You have structure with which to gauge your actions. Even if it is just in reference to a personal goal, context provides a sense of order for what you are observing. This might be as simple as examining your motivations.

Self-observation also pertains to objectivity. Due to inherent difficulties of communication and ability, Tart holds that we fail to make a clear distinction between observer, observation, and observing the observer, yet he points out that the latter is contained in many meditative disciplines. He also advises the development of discriminative awareness by consciously attending to mental processes in such a manner as to separate input from reaction.[28] By paying attention to your thoughts, you stand a better chance of not blindly following them.

The skill of self-observation is therefore that of being conscious of being conscious. The capacity to do this increases corresponding with a decrease in projection-reflection. The more you reflect, the less you observe. As Tart mentions, though, some type of self-referencing is necessary to observe those dynamics. An inability to self-observe in any way ensures dysfunction of many kinds. Imagine watching yourself from a vantage of a few feet away often serves to spark development of this skill.

In addition to self-understanding, self-observation is needed for course corrections, to be able to assess how your behavior matches what is occurring. You need to *see* your behavior to change it. Dishabituation augments this ability.

MANAGING MODELS

Even when you encounter opposition between thoughts, there is always a stable middle ground. Opposites such as external-internal, thesis-antithesis, and predator-prey, are better handled by knowing how to manage the models they originate from. This is the tightrope of life. This is also the remedy to fundamentalism.

The following meditation helps deliver awareness to an in-between point, a place of no tension between opposing points of view. Experiencing balance between two contrary ideas provides direct knowledge that concepts are the building stones of reality, that realities can exist independently of one another, and that it is possible to derive value from not continually referring, and deferring, to a specific reality.

Free Perception

Humans have long struggled with oppositions such as believing we have complete free will or that we have none, with seeing ourselves as cocreators of reality or just observers of that which already is, and thinking that there is no future or that the future is already fixed. If you have deep-seated beliefs regarding any of these concepts, temporarily suspend your beliefs and play for a moment in another sandbox. If you have difficulty forming an image or perception of any step, simply pick a thought or object that somehow relates to the step. I also suggest familiarizing yourself with all of the following steps prior to proceeding.

1. Visualize, feel, or otherwise perceive a sphere of energy representing the beauty of having free will. Immerse yourself in this sphere and allow it to fill your entire being. Your decisions are yours. You have the natural freedom to make your own choices.

2. Place this energy aside for the moment and perceive an energy sphere representing the magnificence of not having free will. You are part and parcel of a divine order and you realize how intimately you are connected with the divine as you perform as an actor on a stage. Your part has already been given to you. Have fun with it.

3. Place both energies before you, equal in distance on each side of the center of your perception. Place your attention in between these energies. Find the balance point—the free perception point—where you are in harmony and feel no tension between the two energies.

4. Leaving that awareness, visualize, feel, or otherwise perceive a sphere of energy representing the brilliance of cocreating your reality. Through give-and-take, you interact with the entire cosmos and your reality is thereby molded.

5. Placing this awareness momentarily aside, perceive an energy sphere representing the power of gradually becoming aware of that which already is. Movement through time and space exists only as an exercise in perception. All time resides in the present and moving through space is the movement of mind. Everything always was and always will be. As you increase your awareness and travel through what we call "time," you gradually become aware of that which already was, is, and always will be.

6. Bring both of these energies to the fore of your awareness. Go in between them to the free perception point.

7. Leaving that awareness, in your own way perceive a sphere of energy representing that there is no future. The future occurs only as a result of what happens in the present. And the present is the present. Future is only a thought.

8. Place this energy aside for the moment and perceive an energy sphere representing the future as already existing. All your actions are preordained. You simply travel through your feelings

to the place where they have already occurred. We are all playing "catch up" to find out what is already there.

9. Place both energies before you and place your attention in
   between them at the free perception point. Notice any and all
   results.

10. Using your imagination, form an equilateral triangle. The three
    points of the triangle represent the free perception points of
    steps 3, 6, and 9.

11. Inside, at the center of the triangle, find the free perception
    point, the place of no tension.

12. At the free perception point notice a speck of white light.
    Approach the white light, which grows larger, more brilliant.
    Place your attention at the threshold of the light.

13. Hold the question "What do I need to learn most at this very
    moment?" in your consciousness. (Feel free to ask anything you
    wish such as "What would be a good learning task?")

14. Leap into the white light. As you do, release your question and
    allow it to flow away from you into the light. Allow the answer
    to return in its own time by any means of perception.

15. Remain in the light as long as you wish. Return when you
    wish.

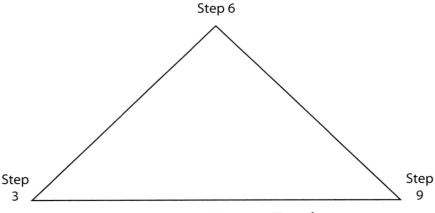

Figure A.1. Free Perception Triangle

A	Balance	B
free will	free perception	no free will
cocreator	free perception	aware of that which is
no future	free perception	future already exists

Notice that the elements of column A and column B are logically consistent. Not only is one secular and the other religious, being a cocreator with the divine follows the thought that you have free will and that you can use your *will* and intent to build your world. In the same manner, becoming aware of that which already is follows from having no free will and that the future is fixed in place. You can add to the elements in each column so long as all of the elements of a column remain consistent and can be related to each other.

When a sufficient number of elements have been brought together, you create a model, perhaps an entire philosophy, and maybe even a reality. These logical systems influence your perception, which influences your behavior, which influences your experiences. Typically, experiences self-validate the philosophy, which places you in a loop where perceptions and experiences are already determined by what and how you think.

Finding the free perception point and using it to move the focal point is one of the more valuable results of commanding this skill. When perception is not hemmed into a point of view, it has greater freedom to move. This cleansing action may also be used as a deliberate step toward mastering imagination; this exercise represents stepping beyond the ordinary into what might be.

Seeing

Seeing is any form of direct perception. It often is a visual sense although it also can be kinesthetic or intuitive. An interesting anomaly is that when you are *seeing* during daylight, the environment becomes dark, and conversely a dark environment becomes light. When I am able to *see* another person's complete energy body, it appears as an oblong ball of light and the surrounding world is comprised of what seems to be long strands of intense yet softly glowing strands of light.

A preliminary to *seeing* is gazing, or opening up. The "Free Perception" exercise is a good place to start. The following steps, here described in relation to *seeing,* can be used to develop any mode of perception. It is also a deautomatization exercise that permits the energies forming cohesion to circulate more freely and thereby allow new perceptions to surface to a conscious level.

1. Relax. Try to be nonattached to anything you perceive. In other words, let go.
2. Establish your intent to gaze.
3. Don't focus on the world as you normally might. Don't pick out an object then look or stare at it. Let your eyes go "soft," unfocused, but with a steady gaze.
4. Feel your body merge with the world. Remain centered within your body as you connect with the external world. Feel the flow of energy.
5. Gazing at shadows is very relaxing. You can use virtually any shadow to gaze at. To elevate the level of skill, create a full pattern of shadows in the same manner you would create a tree out of branches and leaves. In other words, instead of attending to the normal features of leaves, branches, etc., you construct the tree from the shadows within it.
6. If you happen to *see* a haze of light, a thin film of energy, or what looks like swirling dots, let them be. Don't focus on them or you will pull back your prior cohesion and refocus automatically on the ordinary, physical world. The light is the energy world breaking into your awareness; you are *seeing.* Later, when you gain more experience, you will be able to focus on that

energy and it won't disappear. In fact, you will be able to expand that world. But until you train your eyes, and your body, your normal habits of perception will rule.

Seeing automatically removes the influences of models. What you do with your experiences—how you interpret them—is quite another matter. You might end up building elaborate models that end up stopping your growth in its tracks. When *seeing* occurs, let go of habits, including those found in models, to take your skills of orchestrating various energies to the next level.

A BASIC LEARNING POSTURE

All learning and imagination exercises such as those presented here serve to help you manage your energy body. Each shift in cohesion also represents learning, as does working through altered states to a new baseline. Forging a path with heart is one way to make sure that what you learn is purposeful. To help just a bit more, here are behaviors that promote learning. As with anything else, you can keep working to elevate your level of skill.

> *Maintain cool effort.* Don't bash your head into walls. Don't try to force the world into compliance with your wishes. Learn what the world *is*. In addition, don't arbitrarily work according to another person's timetable. Have a little fun finding out the natural rhythms of your life. Then relax, be patient, and let your energy body breathe. Learn to love to learn.
>
> *Exercise a high level of inquiry.* Stay open and flexible. Keep asking questions. Don't settle for an answer when your body yearns for more. Look at the evidence, at what occurred, at what is . . . not what others say is so. Use all of your experience and let your knowledge be rendered obsolete if necessary. Use all the deautomatization skills you can at any time you can. As

the philosopher Arthur Schopenhauer says, "[T]he contempla-
tion and observation of everything *actual,* as soon as it presents something new to the observer, is more instructive than
all reading and hearing about it."[29]

Sustain the pursuit of objectivity. By applying the lessons of the focal
point, we know that anything we perceive is simultaneously real
and illusory: real from its own vantage point; illusory (potential)
from another focal point position. We have objective anatomical
hardware, yet the experience it provides is subjective. Quantum
theory tells us that results are influenced by the observer, which
makes everything subjective. At the same time, this awareness
provides for objectivity. You might say objectivity is what keeps
you from lying to yourself, and to others. It's what allows you to
accurately observe yourself, others, and the world.

Acknowledge complete responsibility. Do so for all your behavior, for
all that you perceive, and for everything that results from your
inquiries and adventures.

Learn for mastery. Prepare yourself to take your learning into new
areas, some of which may cause unwelcome comments from
those who consider themselves authorities. Use the references
provided in this book and on the World Wide Web.

Learning Projects

Learning projects are a way to use habituation in a positive way. By
constant focus on a goal, you build a cohesion, which in turn produces
a new imagining. Once you complete one task, you will have also automatically learned the mechanics of intent.

If you then make your imagining practical, that helps to build a
bridge between learning and imagination. Then the expanse of energy
found in potential takes shape in a workable format. This expands the
first energy field and reduces the second, thereby awakening more of
the energy body. To decide on a task, use your imagination to determine a skill that you have interest in acquiring and one that is also well

beyond your current abilities. An unexpected idea may come to you, something that you had no interest in before. Your task may also seem odd to you in the beginning. Don't worry about the task being right or wrong. The important consideration is to work with the resources of your extended anatomy. Like learning other skills, you'll become more proficient the more you practice.

Castaneda's teammates had projects requiring them to gain proficiency with the practical side of expanded awareness. Their tasks included healing, building using carpentry, and providing solutions to human predicaments.[30] They discovered that, in performing such tasks, individual consciousness meets and exceeds group consensus; that is, the individual both integrates and transcends what is held by the group to be valid. The next phase of the task is to give back to the group.

Once you get a feel for them, learning projects will take you to unforeseen places. Up until the time that I took on the project of writing two books about Castaneda's books, my high school English teachers thought I was hopeless and I passed my classes by the skin of my teeth. I was also thoroughly disenchanted with writing because of this experience, not because I necessarily lacked an innate drive to write. I accepted the writing task don Juan gave me out of respect for him, and I later considered it advantageous to earn a degree in journalism to help fulfill the task. After many years of cultivating the wordsmith part of my nature, writing has become something I am now fairly good at, even earning part of my livelihood from it. I eventually completed my project by publishing two books (under the name Ken Eagle Feather) that provide a shamanic orientation to the properties of the first and second energy fields, respectively.

A new learning task requires that I enter arenas of consciousness that were once literally beyond my imagination. And yet as a child I remember a sense of abounding potential, perhaps, even, of touching infinity. . . .

Notes

PREFACE

1. Under the name Ken Eagle Feather, I have written *Traveling with Power* (Charlottesville, Va.: Hampton Roads Publishing, 1992); *A Toltec Path* (Charlottesville, Va.: Hampton Roads, 1995); retitled *On the Toltec Path* and rereleased as a tenth-anniversary edition (Rochester, Vt.: Bear & Co., 2006); *Tracking Freedom* (Charlottesville, Va.: Hampton Roads, 1998); *The Dream of Vixen Tor* (Charlottesville, Va.: Tracker One Studios, 2001); and *Toltec Dreaming* (Rochester, Vt.: Bear & Co., 2007).

2. Carlos Castaneda, *The Teachings of Don Juan: A Yaqui Way of Knowledge* (New York: Simon & Schuster, 1968).

3. Especially for those who have followed Carlos Castaneda's legacy, it is important to note that contrary to many assertions, his Ph.D. has not been revoked. UCLA Department of Anthropology e-mail correspondence, October 5, 2005.

4. His Holiness the Dalai Lama, *The Universe in a Single Atom: The Convergence of Science and Spirituality* (New York: Morgan Road Books, 2005).

CHAPTER 1. A WORLD OF ENERGY

1. Portions of this section were first published as "Bioenergetics: A New Science of Healing," in *Shift: At the Frontiers of Consciousness,* no. 10, (March–May 2006): 11–13, 34.

2. *American Heritage College Dictionary,* 3rd ed. (Boston: Houghton Mifflin Company, 2000), 139.

3. James Oschman, *Energy Medicine: The Scientific Basis* (Edinburgh, Scotland: Churchill Livingston Press, 2000), 232.

4. Ted J. Kaptchuk, *The Web That Has No Weaver: Understanding Chinese Medicine* (Chicago: Contemporary Books, 2000), 14.

5. Libby Barnett and Maggie Chambers with Susan Davidson, *Reiki Energy Medicine* (Rochester, Vt.: Healing Arts Press, 1996), 20–21.

6. Samuel Hahnemann, *Organon of the Medical Art,* edited by Wenda Brewster O'Reilly (Palo Alto, Calif.: Birdcage Books, 1996), 4, 235–37.

7. Paracelsus Clinic website, www.paracelsus.ch, July 15, 2007.

8. "The Royal Rife Story," www.rifehealth.com, September 30, 2006.

9. Clark A. Manning and Louis J. Vanrenen. *Bioenergetic Medicines East and West: Acupuncture and Homeopathy* (Berkeley, Calif.: North Atlantic Books, 1988), 9.

10. Oschman, *Energy Medicine,* 76–79; Hong-Chang Yang, Jau-Han Chen, Shu-Yun Wang, Chin-Hao Chen, Jen-Tzong Jeng, Ji-Cheng Chen, Chiu-Hsien Wu, Shu-Hsien Liao, and Herng-Er Horng, "Superconducting Quantum Interference Device: The Most Sensitive Detector of Magnetic Flux," *Tamkang Journal of Science and Engineeering* 6, no. 1 (2003): 9–18; and Takenaka Corporation website, www.takenaka.co.jp./takenaka_e/techno/19_sldrm/19_sldrm.htm, August 16, 2007.

11. Dr. Korotkov Co. website, www.korotkov.org, August 18, 2007.

12. PIP Bio Imaging website, www.pipbiofieldimaging.com, September 12, 2007; The Centre for Biofield Sciences website, www.biofieldsciences.com, September 15, 2007; and presentation by Brian Daily, MD, at a conference sponsored by the Institute for Therapeutic Discovery, September 8, 2007.

13. Alexander Lowen, *Bioenergetics* (New York: Penguin Arkana, 1994).

14. Fred P. Gallo, *Energy Psychology: Explorations at the Interface of Energy, Cognition, Behavior, and Health* (Boca Raton, Fla.: CRC Press, 1999).

15. University of Colorado at Colorado Springs website, http://w.uccs.edu/rjones, August 1, 2005.

16. As of the writing of this book, I was employed by the Institute for Therapeutic Discovery (www.tiftd.org) and provided consulting services to Beech Tree Labs, Inc. (www.beechtreelabs.com).

17. Larry Dossey, *Reinventing Medicine: Beyond Mind-Body to a New Era of Healing* (New York: HarperCollins, 1999), 27, 58–59; and Marilyn Schlitz and William Braud, "Distant Intentionality and Healing: Assessing the Evidence," *Alternative Therapies* 3, no. 6 (November 1997): 62–73.

18. James Oschman, "Energy and the Healing Response," *Journal of Bodywork and Movement Therapies* 9 (2005): 3–15.

19. Oschman, *Energy Medicine,* 11.

20. James Oschman, e-mail interviews, May 19, 2005, and June 11, 2005.

21. Milo Wolff, e-mail interview, October 14 and 15, 2005.

22. Institute of Transpersonal Psychology website, www.itp.edu, October 2, 2005.

23. Stuart R. Hameroff, Alfred W. Kaszniak, and Alwyn C. Scott, eds. *Toward a Science of Consciousness: The Tucson Discussions and Debates* (Cambridge, Mass.: The MIT Press, 1996, 1998, 1999).

24. Abraham H. Maslow, *Toward a Psychology of Being,* 3rd ed. (New York: John Wiley & Sons, 1999), 85.

25. Paul Pearsall, *The Beethoven Factor: The New Positive Psychology of Hardiness, Happiness, Healing, and Hope* (Charlottesville, Va.: Hampton Roads Publishing Co., 2003), 203–19.

26. Published by Simon & Schuster and its imprint Washington Square Press, Carlos Castaneda wrote *The Teachings of Don Juan* (1968), *A Separate Reality* (1971), *Journey to Ixtlan* (1972), *Tales of Power* (1974), *The Second Ring of Power* (1977), *The Eagle's Gift* (1981), *The Fire from Within* (1984), and *The Power of Silence* (1987). HarperCollins then published *The Art of Dreaming* (1993) and *The Active Side of Infinity* (1998).

27. Many of the terms in this book are taken from, or related to, those in Castaneda's books. In this instance, I changed his term of "assemblage point" to the "focal point" and have added "core" as a distinct function of the energy body.

28. My term, "learning" applies to what Castaneda referred to as "stalking." As with my prior books, I find that this term carries too much of a negative connotation. "Imagination," in turn, is what Castaneda referred to as "dreaming."

29. Violet S. de Laslo, ed., R. F. C. Hull, trans., *The Basic Writings of C. G. Jung* (Princeton, N.J.: Princeton University Press, 1990), 147–48; and Maslow, *Psychology of Being,* 20, 32.

30. A. R. Lacey, *A Dictionary of Philosophy* (New York: Barnes & Noble Books, 1996), 205; and Dagobert Runes, *Dictionary of Philosophy* (Totowa, N.J.: Littlefield, Adams, and Co., 1980), 219.

31. Andrew M. Colman, *A Dictionary of Psychology* (Oxford: Oxford University Press, 2001), 600.

32. Sally P. Springer and Georg Deutsch, *Left Brain, Right Brain,* 4th ed. (New York: W. H. Freeman and Co., 1993), 272; and Richard M. Restak, *The Brain: The Last Frontier* (New York: Warner Books, 1979), 49–71.

33. Carlos Castaneda, *The Power of Silence* (New York: Washington Square Press, 1987), 155–90; Castaneda's teacher, don Juan Matus, often cited "losing self-importance" as a key maneuver for learning. For immediate reference, see chapter 3 in Castaneda's *Journey to Ixtlan.* "Stopping internal dialogue" is also cited throughout his works as a principle exercise.

CHAPTER 2. ANATOMY OF THE ENERGY BODY

1. Oschman, *Energy Medicine,* 74, 206, 209.

2. Robert M. Berne, Matthew N. Levy, Bruce M. Koeppen, and Bruce A. Stanton, eds., *Physiology,* 4th ed. (St. Louis: Mosby, 1998), 653.

3. James Austin, *Zen and the Brain: Toward an Understanding of Meditation and Consciousness* (Cambridge, Mass.: MIT Press, 1999), 83–88; and Bruce Lipton, *The Biology of Belief* (Santa Rosa, Calif.: Elite Books, 2005), 163–65.

4. Robert O. Becker and Gary Selden, *The Body Electric: Electromagnetism and the Foundation of Life* (New York: William Morrow, 1985); Oschman, *Energy Medicine,* 61.

5. International Association for Biologically Closed Circuits website, www.iabc.readywebsites.com, September 22, 2006.

6. World Health Organization, *Standard Acupuncture Nomenclature,* 2nd ed. (Manila: WHO Regional Office, 1993).

7. Kaptchuk, *The Web That Has No Weaver,* 41–74.

8. Ibid., 75–104.

9. Caroline Myss, *Anatomy of the Spirit: The Seven Stages of Power and Healing* (New York: Harmony Books, 1996), 69.

10. Nadi (yoga), http://en.wikipedia.org, December 14, 2007.

11. Milo Wolff, e-mail correspondence, October 14, 2005.

12. Castaneda, *The Fire from Within*, 50.

13. Christopher J. Conselice, "The Universe's Invisible Hand," *Scientific American* (February 2007): 35–41.

14. James Oschman, e-mail correspondence, September 10, 2005.

15. Barbara Ann Brennan, *Hands of Light: A Guide to Healing through the Human Energy Field* (New York: Bantam, 1987).

16. Castaneda, *The Fire from Within*, 157–59.

17. Ibid., 108.

18. Jon Whale, *The Catalyst of Power: The Assemblage Point of Man* (Findhorn, Scotland: Findhorn Press, 2001). Whale successfully demonstrated the viability of both technologies during a workshop I gave in England in the late 1990s.

19. Castaneda, *The Power of Silence*, 6–7.

20. Castaneda, *The Fire from Within*, 83.

21. Castaneda, *Tales of Power*, 95–96.

22. Oschman, *Energy Medicine*, 29.

23. Daniel Goleman, *Emotional Intelligence* (New York: Bantam Books, 1995), 83–86, 136–38.

24. Valerie V. Hunt, *Infinite Mind: Science of the Human Vibrations of Consciousness* (Malibu, Calif.: Malibu Publishing, 1996), 104–31; Antonio Damasio, *The Feeling of What Happens: Body and Emotion in the Making of Consciousness* (New York: Harcourt Brace and Company, 1999), 41; Candace Pert, *Molecules of Emotion* (New York: Scribner, 1997); and Candace Pert, "Molecules and Choice," *Shift: At the Frontiers of Consciousness* (September–November 2004): 21.

25. Castaneda, *Tales of Power*, 95.

26. Arthur Schopenhauer, E. F. J. Payne, ed., *The World as Will and Representation*, vols. 1, 2 (New York: Dover Publications, 1969).

27. IBS Research Update website, www.ibs-research-update.org.uk, September 22, 2006.

28. De Laslo, *Basic Writings*, 41–43.

29. Ibid., 56.

30. Ibid., 59.

31. Ibid., 43, 57, 140.

32. Ibid., 59, 122.

33. Castaneda, *The Fire from Within*, xiii.

CHAPTER 3. CONSTRUCTING REALITY

1. Entrainment references, http://en.wikipedia.org, October 2, 2006.

2. Irving M. Copi, *Introduction to Logic,* 6th ed. (New York: Macmillan, 1982), 99–105.

3. Damasio, *Feeling of What Happens,* 308.

4. Castaneda, *The Fire from Within,* 176, 213.

5. The Quotations Page website, www.quotationspage.com, December 10, 2006.

6. Castaneda, *The Art of Dreaming,* 22; and Eagle Feather, *Toltec Dreaming,* 94.

7. Colman, *Dictionary of Psychology,* 404.

8. Glen O. Gabbard and Stuart Twemlow, *With the Eyes of the Mind: An Empirical Analysis of Out-of-Body States* (New York: Praeger, 1984), 150.

9. Castaneda, *The Art of Dreaming,* 142.

10. Eagle Feather, *Toltec Dreaming,* 44; and Joseph McMoneagle, *Mind Trek: Exploring Consciousness, Time, and Space through Remote Viewing* (Charlottesville, Va.: Hampton Roads Publishing Co., 1997), 15.

11. Arnold Mindell, *Dreaming While Awake: Techniques for 24-Hour Lucid Dreaming* (Charlottesville, Va.: Hampton Roads Publishing Co., 2000), 6.

12. Maslow, *Psychology of Being,* 85.

13. De Laslo, *Basic Writings,* 148.

14. Abraham H. Maslow, *Maslow on Management* (New York: John Wiley & Sons, 1998), xx.

15. Richard Gerber, *Vibrational Medicine* (Rochester, Vt.: Bear & Co., 2001), 17.

16. Catherine Arnst, "Biotech, Finally," *BusinessWeek* (June 13, 2005): 30.

17. Henry Petroski, *Design Paradigms: Case Histories of Error and Judgment in Engineering* (Cambridge, UK: Cambridge University Press, 1994), 1–2.

18. Lionel R. Milgrom, "Entanglement, Knowledge, and Their Possible Effects on the Outcomes of Blinded Trials of Homeopathic Provings," *Journal of Alternative and Complementary Medicine* 12, no. 3 (2006): 271–79.

19. Oschman, *Energy Medicine,* 154.

20. Thomas S. Kuhn, *The Structure of Scientific Revolutions,* 3rd ed. (Chicago: University of Chicago Press, 1996), 77–82.

CHAPTER 4. EXPANDING THE BOUNDARIES

1. Charles T. Tart, *States of Consciousness* (Lincoln, Neb.: www.iUniverse.com, Inc., 2000), 5–9.

2. Castaneda, *The Fire from Within,* 23.

3. Maslow, *Psychology of Being,* 31–33, 170–75.

4. Castaneda, *The Fire from Within,* 50.

5. Seymour H. Mauskopf and Michael R. McVaugh, *The Elusive Science: Origins of Experimental Psychical Research* (Baltimore, Md.: Johns Hopkins University Press, 1980), 5, 169; and Charles T. Tart, *Open Mind, Discriminating Mind: Reflections on Human Possibilities* (Lincoln, Neb.: www.iUniverse.com, Inc., 2000), 61, 76–82, 85.

6. Mauskopf and McVaugh, *Elusive Science,* 3, 13.

7. Gabbard and Twemlow, *Eyes of the Mind,* 15–23.

8. Joseph McMoneagle, *Memoirs of a Psychic Spy: The Remarkable Life of U.S. Government Remote Viewer 001,* (Charlottesville, Va.: Hampton Roads Publishing Co., 2006), xi–xii; and personal conversations with Joseph McMoneagle and a client during 2005–2006.

9. Brian Greene, *The Fabric of the Cosmos: Space, Time, and the Texture of Reality* (New York: Alfred A. Knopf, 2005), 11–12.

10. Philip C. Almond, *Mystical Experience and Religious Doctrine: An Investigation of the Study of Mysticism in World Religions* (Berlin: Mouton Publishers, 1982), 122–23.

11. Fritjof Capra, *The Tao of Physics: An Exploration of the Parallels between Modern Physics and Eastern Mysticism* (Boston: Shambhala, 2000), 52–54.

12. Hunt, *Infinite Mind,* 163.

13. William James, *The Varieties of Religious Experience* (New York: New American Library, 1958), 292–94.

14. Maslow, *Psychology of Being,* 93–106.

15. Runes, *Dictionary of Philosophy,* 203.

16. P. D. Ouspensky, *The Fourth Way* (New York: Vintage Books, 1971), 97–104.

17. Charles T. Tart, ed., *Altered States of Consciousness,* rev. ed. (New York: HarperSanFrancisco, 1990), 581–99.

18. Jack Kornfield, *A Path with Heart: A Guide through the Perils and Promises of Spiritual Life* (New York: Bantam Books, 1993), 120–22.

19. Almond, *Mystical Experience,* 69–91.

20. Leah Buturain, "Materializing the Mystery: Body Imagery in Catholic Visual Culture," presented at the Luce Colloquium, Fuller Seminar, February 16, 2005.

21. Robert Monroe, *Journeys Out of the Body* (New York: Doubleday, 1971).

22. Springer and Deutsch, *Left Brain, Right Brain,* 1–17, 272.

23. F. Holmes Atwater, "The Hemi-Sync® Process," Monroe Institute Research Division, June 1999.

24. Raymond Moody, *Life After Life* (Harrisburg, Penn.: Stackpole Books, 1976), 29–49; Gabbard and Twemlow, *Eyes of the Mind,* 136–38.

25. Eagle Feather, *Toltec Dreaming,* 76–77.

26. Marcus Chown, *The Universe Next Door: The Making of Tomorrow's Science* (Oxford: Oxford University Press, 2002), 25–26.

27. Paul J. Nahin, *Time Travel* (Cincinnati, Ohio: Writer's Digest Books, 1997), 167–68.

28. Michio Kaku, *Hyperspace: A Scientific Odyssey through Parallel Universes, Time Warps, and the 10th Dimension* (New York: Anchor Books, 1994), 15–16; and James Trefil, ed., *Encyclopedia of Science and Technology* (New York: Routledge, 2001), 463–64.

29. Kaku, *Hyperspace,* 49–51.

CHAPTER 5. REFLECTION AND PROJECTION

1. Reber, *Dictionary of Psychology,* 570.

2. Tart, *States of Consciousness,* 264.

3. Martin Heidegger, trans., John Macquarrie and Edward Robinson, *Being and Time* (San Francisco: HarperSanFrancisco, 1962), 371, 414.

4. Arthur J. Deikman, "Deautomatization and the Mystic Experience," Tart, ed., *Altered States,* 34–57.

5. Tart, *States of Consciousness,* 117.

6. Castaneda, *The Fire from Within,* 154.

7. Shunryu Suzuki, *Zen Mind, Beginner's Mind* (New York: Weatherhill, 1973), 116–17.

8. Hunt, *Infinite Mind,* 104–11.

9. Austin, *Zen and the Brain,* 227.

10. Castaneda, *Teachings,* 82–87; and Eagle Feather, *Toltec Path,* 113–22.

11. Castaneda, *The Fire from Within,* 118.

12. Ibid., 108.
13. Castaneda, *Teachings,* 86.
14. Ibid., 87.
15. This esoteric ability is beyond the scope of this work. You may read more about it in Ken Eagle Feather's *Toltec Dreaming,* or in Carlos Castaneda's *The Fire from Within.*
16. Eagle Feather, *Toltec Path,* 109–13.
17. Ibid.

CHAPTER 6. THE NATURE OF FUNDAMENTALISM

1. Barnett and Chambers, *Reiki Energy,* 2.
2. Arthur S. Reber and Emily Reber, eds., *The Penguin Dictionary of Psychology,* 3rd ed. (London: Penguin Books, 1995), 125.
3. Elliot Dacher, *Integral Health: The Path to Human Flourishing* (Laguna Beach, Calif.: Basic Health Publications, Inc., 2006), 139–46.
4. Maslow, *Psychology of Being,* 39–41.
5. Patrick Bernhagen, "Power: Making Sense of an Elusive Concept," presented at Trinity College Dublin, 2002.
6. Gerald M. Edelman, *Second Nature: Brain Science and Human Knowledge* (New Haven, Conn.: Yale University Press, 2006), 95.
7. Maslow, *Psychology of Being,* 20.
8. Eagle Feather, *Toltec Path,* 110.
9. John Horgan, *Rational Mysticism: Dispatches from the Border between Science and Spirituality* (New York: Houghton Mifflin Company, 2003), 118–19.
10. Paul E. Johnson, *Psychology of Religion, Revised* (Nashville, Tenn.: Abingdon Press, 1959), 223–26.
11. De Laslo, *Basic Writings,* 54–55.
12. Maslow, *Psychology of Being,* 166–73.
13. Johnson, *Psychology of Religion,* 104, 220.
14. Castaneda, *The Fire from Within,* 74–75.
15. Ibid., 176.
16. Castaneda, *Art of Dreaming,* 104; and Arthur Deikman, *The Wrong Way Home: Uncovering the Patterns of Cult Behavior in America* (Boston: Beacon Press, 1990), 96.

17. Deikman, *Wrong Way Home,* 101, 105.

18. John Van Auken, "Guides, Angels, and the Holy One," *Venture Inward* 10, no. 6 (July/August 1994).

CHAPTER 7. A CREATIVE LIFE

1. Goleman, *Emotional Intelligence,* 43–44.

2. Howard Gardner, *Frames of Mind: The Theory of Multiple Intelligences* (New York: HarperCollins, 1983), xii, xviii.

3. J. P. Chaplin, *Dictionary of Psychology* (New York: Dell Publishing, 1975), 263.

4. Gardner, *Frames of Mind,* 60, 68.

5. Thomas Donaldson and Patricia H. Werhane, eds., *Ethical Issues in Business: A Philosophical Approach,* 5th ed. (Upper Saddle River, N.J.: Prentice Hall, 1996), 3–11.

6. *American Heritage Dictionary,* 284.

7. Castaneda, *A Separate Reality,* 20–23.

8. Castaneda, *The Active Side,* 179.

9. Castaneda, *The Fire from Within,* xii.

10. Johann Christoph Arnold, *Why Forgive?* (Farmington, Penn.: Plough Publishing House, 2000).

11. Castaneda, *The Art of Dreaming,* 73.

12. Castaneda, *The Power of Silence,* 82.

13. Castaneda, *Tales of Power,* 58.

14. Castaneda, *The Teachings of Don Juan,* 87.

15. Sidney Spencer, *Mysticism in World Religion* (Gloucester, Mass.: Peter Smith, 1971), 47–66.

16. Castaneda, *The Art of Dreaming,* 75; *Tales of Power,* 294.

17. Castaneda, *The Fire from Within,* 159–60.

18. His Holiness the Dalai Lama, *Ethics for the New Millennium* (New York: Riverhead, 1999), 161–71.

19. Richard Sennett, *The Corrosion of Character: The Personal Consequences of Work in the New Capitalism* (New York: W. W. Norton & Company, 1998), 10–11, 28–29, 104.

20. Castaneda, *Journey to Ixtlan,* 43.

21. Castaneda, *Tales of Power,* 287.

22. J. C. Cooper, *Taoism: The Way of the Mystic* (York Beach, Maine: Samuel Weiser, Inc., 1972), 20.

23. Maslow, *On Management,* 205.

24. Castaneda, *The Fire from Within,* 138.

25. Ibid., 14, 80.

26. Ibid., 110, 119; Castaneda, *The Art of Dreaming,* 33.

27. Castaneda, *The Fire from Within,* 14.

28. Cooper, *Taoism,* 13, 85–86.

29. Milo Wolff, "Einstein's Last Question," *Temple University Frontier Perspectives* (Spring 2005).

30. J. Adriaan Bouwknecht, Francesca Spiga, Daniel R. Staub, Matthew W. Hale, Anantha Shekhar, and Christopher A. Lowry, "Differential effects of exposure to low-light or high-light open-field on anxiety-related behaviors: Relationship to c-Fos expression in serotonergic and non-serotonergic neurons in the dorsal raphe nucleus," *Brain Research Bulletin* 72, no. 1 (April 2, 2007): 32–43.

31. Lipton, *Biology of Belief,* 15–27, 49–73.

32. Donaldson and Werhane, *Ethical Issues,* 424–58.

33. Michael Lerner, *Spirit Matters* (Charlottesville, Va.: Hampton Roads Publishing, 2000), 138–64.

34. Maslow, *Psychology of Being,* 39–41, 175–76, 197–205.

35. Lipton, *Biology of Belief,* 26–27.

36. Lionel R. Milgrom, "Entanglement, Knowledge, and Their Possible Effects on the Outcomes of Blinded Trials of Homeopathic Provings," *Journal of Alternative and Complementary Medicine* 12, no. 3 (2006): 271–79.

37. Oschman, *Energy Medicine,* 175–86, 201–3.

38. David W. Sollars, *The Complete Idiot's Guide to Acupuncture & Acupressure* (New York: Alpha Books, 2000), 25.

39. Hahnemann, *Organon,* 224.

40. Hunt, *Infinite Mind,* 9–36.

41. Castaneda, *The Fire from Within,* 49, 57.

42. Castaneda, *The Art of Dreaming,* 45; *The Fire from Within,* 109.

43. David Darling, *Teleportation: The Impossible Leap* (Hoboken, N.J.: John Wiley & Sons, 2005), 168–88.

44. Neil A. Stillings, Steven E. Weisler, Christopher H. Chase, Mark H. Feinstein, Jay L. Garfield, and Edwina L. Rissland, *Cognitive Science,* 2nd ed. (Cambridge, Mass.: MIT Press, 1995), 55–63.

45. Castaneda, *The Power of Silence,* 29–32.
46. Dalai Lama, *Ethics,* 219–21.
47. Johnson, *Psychology of Religion,* 102.
48. Leon R. Kass, *Life, Liberty and the Defense of Dignity: The Challenge of Bioethics* (San Francisco: Encounter Books, 2002) 8–12, 29–49.
49. James F. Drane, *More Humane Medicine: A Liberal Catholic Bioethic* (Edinboro, Penn.: Edinboro University Press, 2003), 1–6.
50. Mastery Learning references: Thomas H. Allen, Humboldt State University, www.humboldt.edu/~that1/mastery.html; www.funderstanding.com/mastery_learning.cfm, May 30, 2007; and http://en.wikipedia.org, December 6, 2007.
51. Kornfield, *Path with Heart.*
52. Castaneda, *Ixtlan,* 26–35.
53. Eagle Feather, *Toltec Path,* 170–72.
54. Stephen Levine, *A Year to Live: How to Live This Year As If It Were Your Last* (New York: Bell Tower, 1997), 39–40, 52.
55. Pearsall, *Beethoven Factor,* 7–19, 31.

CHAPTER 8. THE UNFOLDING MOMENT

1. Heidegger, *Being and Time,* 22–23.
2. Ibid., 78, 415–18.
3. Ibid., 12, 85–94.
4. Ibid., 130–37.
5. Maslow, *Psychology of Being,* 169.
6. Ibid., 170, 222.
7. Castaneda, *The Fire from Within,* 4–5, 147–48.
8. Castaneda, *Tales of Power,* 97–98.
9. Jones, *Physics,* 212–216.
10. Mihaly Csikszentmihalyi, *Flow: The Psychology of Optimal Experience* (New York: Harper Perennial, 1990), xi.
11. Goleman, *Emotional Intelligence,* 90.
12. Michael Murphy and Rhea A. White, *In the Zone: The Transcendent Experience in Sports* (New York: Penguin Books, 1995), 149–50.
13. Heidegger, *Being and Time,* 411–15.
14. Castaneda, *The Fire from Within,* 23.

15. Ibid., 170–71.

16. Ibid., 171.

17. Csikszentmihalyi, *Flow,* 26.

18. Ibid., 27.

19. Castaneda, *A Separate Reality,* 84.

20. Goleman, *Emotional Intelligence,* 62, 21.

21. Ibid., 293.

22. Colman, *Dictionary of Psychology,* 369, 379.

23. Malcolm Gladwell, *Blink: The Power of Thinking without Thinking* (New York: Back Bay Books, 2005), 107.

24. Castaneda, *The Fire from Within,* 168–69.

25. Eric R. Kandel, James R. Schwartz, and Thomas M. Jessell, eds., *Principles of Neural Science,* 4th ed. (New York: McGraw-Hill, 2000), 388–92.

26. Russell Targ and Jane Katra, *Miracles of Mind: Exploring Nonlocal Consciousness and Spiritual Healing* (Novato, Calif.: New World Library, 1998), 251.

27. Albert Einstein, *Ideas and Opinions* (New York: Three Rivers Press, 1982), 226.

28. Castaneda, *The Power of Silence,* 14.

29. David G. Myers, "The Powers and Perils of Intuition: Understanding the Nature of Our Gut Instincts," *Scientific American Mind* (June/July 2007): 24–29.

30. Jerome Groopman, *How Doctors Think* (Boston: Houghton Mifflin, 2007), 44.

31. Suzuki, *Zen Mind,* 21.

32. Julian Jaynes, *The Origins of Consciousness in the Breakdown of the Bicameral Mind* (Boston: Houghton Mifflin, 1990), 236–46.

33. Eagle Feather, *Toltec Dreaming,* 139–42.

34. Tart, *Open Mind,* 182–83.

35. Sharon Begley, "How the Brain Rewires Itself," *Time* (January 29, 2007): 79.

36. Targ and Katra, *Miracles,* 257.

37. Castaneda, *A Separate Reality,* 153.

APPENDIX: ENERGY MANAGEMENT SKILLS

1. Castaneda, *Ixtlan,* 181–99.

2. Castaneda, *The Fire from Within,* 131.

3. Tart, *States of Consciousness,* 117.

4. Castaneda, *The Fire from Within,* 148.

5. Ibid., 154.

6. Castaneda, *A Separate Reality,* 91.

7. Castaneda, *Ixtlan,* 18–19; and Eagle Feather, *Toltec Dreaming,* 175–76.

8. Castaneda, *Ixtlan,* 59–70, 88–104.

9. Ibid., 70.

10. Goleman, *Emotional Intelligence,* 65.

11. Tart, *Open Mind,* 225.

12. Oschman, *Energy Medicine,* 111–15.

13. Taisha Abelar, *The Sorcerer's Crossing: A Woman's Journey* (New York: Penguin Arkana, 1992), 42–65; Castaneda, *Eagle's Gift,* 285–89; Eagle Feather, *Toltec Dreaming,* 185–88; and Victor Sanchez, *The Toltec Path of Recapitulation: Healing Your Past to Free Your Soul* (Rochester, Vt.: Bear & Company, 2001).

14. Tart, *Open Mind,* 187–88.

15. Suzuki, *Zen Mind,* 29–31.

16. Barnett and Chambers, *Reiki,* 43.

17. Herbert Benson with Miriam Z. Klipper, *The Relaxation Response* (New York: Harper, 2000), xvi.

18. Tart, *Open Mind,* 39, 247–50.

19. Tart, *States of Consciousness,* 25.

20. Gallo, *Energy Psychology,* 4.

21. Castaneda, *The Power of Silence,* 220.

22. Castaneda, *The Teachings of Don Juan,* 106–7.

23. Suzuki, *Zen Mind,* 119–21.

24. Tart, *States of Consciousness,* 280–81.

25. Castaneda, *A Separate Reality,* 151.

26. Donald B. Calne, *Within Reason: Rationality and Human Behavior* (New York: Pantheon Books, 1999), 243.

27. Ouspensky, *Fourth Way,* 159, 258, 310.

28. Tart, *States of Consciousness,* 156–62, 278.

29. Schopenhauer, *World as Will,* vol. 2, 72.

30. Castaneda, *The Eagle's Gift,* 54.

Bibliography

Abelar, Taisha. *The Sorcerer's Crossing: A Woman's Journey.* New York: Penguin Arkana, 1992.

Almond, Philip C. *Mystical Experience and Religious Doctrine: An Investigation of the Study of Mysticism in World Religions.* Berlin: Mouton Publishers, 1982.

American Heritage College Dictionary, 3rd ed. Boston: Houghton Mifflin Company, 2000.

Arnold, Johann Christoph. *Why Forgive?* Farmington, Penn.: Plough Publishing House, 2000.

Austin, James. *Zen and the Brain: Toward an Understanding of Meditation and Consciousness.* Cambridge, Mass.: MIT Press, 1999.

Barnett, Libby, and Maggie Chambers, with Susan Davidson. *Reiki Energy Medicine.* Rochester, Vt.: Healing Arts Press, 1996.

Becker, Robert O., and Gary Selden. *The Body Electric: Electromagnetism and the Foundation of Life.* New York: William Morrow, 1985.

Benson, Herbert with Miriam Z. Klipper. *The Relaxation Response.* New York: Harper, 2000.

Berne, Robert M., Matthew N. Levy, Bruce M. Koeppen, and Bruce A. Stanton, eds. *Physiology,* 4th ed. St. Louis: Mosby, 1998.

Brennan, Barbara Ann. *Hands of Light: A Guide to Healing through the Human Energy Field.* New York: Bantam, 1987.

Calne, Donald B. *Within Reason: Rationality and Human Behavior.* New York: Pantheon Books, 1999.

Capra, Fritjof. *The Tao of Physics: An Exploration of the Parallels between Modern Physics and Eastern Mysticism*. Boston: Shambhala, 2000.

Castaneda, Carlos. *The Active Side of Infinity*. New York: HarperCollins, 1998.

———. *The Art of Dreaming*. New York: HarperCollins, 1993.

———. *The Eagle's Gift*. New York: Washington Square Press, 1981.

———. *The Fire from Within*. New York: Washington Square Press, 1984.

———. *Journey to Ixtlan: The Lessons of Don Juan*. New York: Washington Square Press, 1972.

———. *The Power of Silence: Further Lessons of Don Juan*. New York: Washington Square Press, 1987.

———. *A Separate Reality: Further Conversations with Don Juan*. New York: Washington Square Press, 1971.

———. *The Second Ring of Power*. New York: Washington Square Press, 1977.

———. *Tales of Power*. New York: Washington Square Press, 1974.

———. *The Teachings of Don Juan: A Yaqui Way of Knowledge*. New York: Washington Square Press, 1968.

Chaplin, J. P. *Dictionary of Psychology*. New York: Dell Publishing, 1975.

Chown, Marcus. *The Universe Next Door: The Making of Tomorrow's Science*. Oxford: Oxford University Press, 2002.

Colman, Andrew M. *A Dictionary of Psychology*. Oxford: Oxford University Press, 2001.

Cooper, J. C. *Taoism: The Way of the Mystic*. York Beach, Maine: Samuel Weiser, Inc., 1972.

Copi, Irving M. *Introduction to Logic,* 6th ed. New York: Macmillan, 1982.

Csikszentmihalyi, Mihaly. *Flow: The Psychology of Optimal Experience*. New York: Harper Perennial, 1990.

Dacher, Elliot. *Integral Health: The Path to Human Flourishing*. Laguna Beach, Calif.: Basic Health Publications, Inc., 2006.

Dalai Lama, His Holiness the. *Ethics for the New Millennium*. New York: Riverhead, 1999.

———. *The Universe in a Single Atom: The Convergence of Science and Spirituality*. New York: Morgan Road Books, 2005.

Damasio, Antonio. *The Feeling of What Happens: Body and Emotion in the Making of Consciousness*. New York: Harcourt Brace and Company, 1999.

Darling, David. *Teleportation: The Impossible Leap.* Hoboken, N.J.: John Wiley & Sons, 2005.

De Laslo, Violet S., ed., Hull, R. F. C., trans., *The Basic Writings of C. G. Jung.* Princeton, N.J.: Princeton University Press, 1990.

Deikman, Arthur. *The Wrong Way Home: Uncovering the Patterns of Cult Behavior in America.* Boston: Beacon Press, 1990.

Donaldson, Thomas, and Werhane, Patricia H., eds. *Ethical Issues in Business: A Philosophical Approach,* 5th ed. Upper Saddle River, N.J.: Prentice Hall, 1996.

Dossey, Larry. *Reinventing Medicine: Beyond Mind-Body to a New Era of Healing.* New York: HarperCollins, 1999.

Drane, James F. *More Humane Medicine: A Liberal Catholic Bioethic.* Edinboro, Penn.: Edinboro University Press, 2003.

Edelman, Gerald M. *Second Nature: Brain Science and Human Knowledge.* New Haven, Conn.: Yale University Press, 2006.

Einstein, Albert. *Ideas and Opinions.* New York: Three Rivers Press, 1982.

Feather, Ken Eagle. *The Dream of Vixen Tor.* Charlottesville, Va.: Tracker One Studios, 2001.

———. *On the Toltec Path: A User's Guide to the Teachings of Don Juan Matus, Carlos Castaneda, and Other Toltec Seers.* Rochester, Vt.: Bear & Co., 2006.

———. *Toltec Dreaming: Don Juan's Teachings on the Energy Body.* Rochester, Vt.: Bear & Co., 2007.

———. *Tracking Freedom: A Guide for Personal Evolution.* Charlottesville, Va.: Hampton Roads Publishing Co., 1998.

———. *Traveling with Power: The Exploration and Development of Perception.* Charlottesville, Va.: Hampton Roads Publishing Co., 1992.

Gabbard, Glen O., and Stuart Twemlow. *With the Eyes of the Mind: An Empirical Analysis of Out-of-Body States.* New York: Praeger, 1984.

Gallo, Fred P. *Energy Psychology: Explorations at the Interface of Energy, Cognition, Behavior, and Health.* Boca Raton, Fla.: CRC Press, 1999.

Gardner, Howard. *Frames of Mind: The Theory of Multiple Intelligences.* New York: HarperCollins, 1983.

Gerber, Richard. *Vibrational Medicine.* Rochester, Vt.: Bear & Co., 2001.

Gladwell, Malcolm. *Blink: The Power of Thinking without Thinking.* New York: Back Bay Books, 2005.

Goleman, Daniel. *Emotional Intelligence.* New York: Bantam Books, 1995.

Greene, Brian. *The Fabric of the Cosmos: Space, Time, and the Texture of Reality.* New York: Alfred A. Knopf, 2005.

Groopman, Jerome. *How Doctors Think.* Boston: Houghton Mifflin, 2007.

Hahnemann, Samuel. *Organon of the Medical Art.* Edited by Wenda Brewster O'Reilly. Palo Alto, Calif.: Birdcage Books, 1996.

Hameroff, Stuart R., Alfred W. Kaszniak, and Alwyn C. Scott, eds. *Toward a Science of Consciousness: The Tucson Discussions and Debates.* Cambridge, Mass.: The MIT Press, 1996, 1998, 1999.

Heidegger, Martin. *Being and Time.* Translated by John Macquarrie and Edward Robinson. HarperSanFrancisco, 1962.

Horgan, John. *Rational Mysticism: Dispatches from the Border between Science and Spirituality.* New York: Houghton Mifflin Company, 2003.

Hunt, Valerie V. *Infinite Mind: Science of the Human Vibrations of Consciousness.* Malibu, Calif.: Malibu Publishing, 1996.

James, William. *The Varieties of Religious Experience.* New York: New American Library, 1958.

Jaynes, Julian. *The Origins of Consciousness in the Breakdown of the Bicameral Mind.* Boston: Houghton Mifflin, 1990.

Johnson, Paul E. *Psychology of Religion, Revised.* Nashville, Tenn.: Abingdon Press, 1959.

Kaku, Michio. *Hyperspace: A Scientific Odyssey through Parallel Universes, Time Warps, and the 10th Dimension.* New York: Anchor Books, 1994.

Kandel, Eric R., James H. Schwartz, and Thomas M. Jessell, eds. *Principles of Neural Science,* 4th ed. New York: McGraw-Hill, 2000.

Kaptchuk, Ted J. *The Web That Has No Weaver: Understanding Chinese Medicine.* Chicago: Contemporary Books, 2000.

Kass, Leon R. *Life, Liberty and the Defense of Dignity: The Challenge of Bioethics.* San Francisco: Encounter Books, 2002.

Kornfield, Jack. *A Path with Heart: A Guide through the Perils and Promises of Spiritual Life.* New York: Bantam Books, 1993.

Kuhn, Thomas S. *The Structure of Scientific Revolutions,* 3rd ed. Chicago: University of Chicago Press, 1996.

Lacey, A. R. *A Dictionary of Philosophy.* New York: Barnes & Noble Books, 1996.

Lerner, Michael. *Spirit Matters*. Charlottesville, Va.: Hampton Roads Publishing, 2000.

Levine, Stephen. *A Year to Live: How to Live This Year As If It Were Your Last*. New York: Bell Tower, 1997.

Lipton, Bruce. *The Biology of Belief: Unleashing the Power of Consciousness, Matter, and Miracles*. Santa Rosa, Calif.: Elite Books, 2005.

Lowen, Alexander. *Bioenergetics*. New York: Penguin Arkana, 1994.

Manning, Clark A., and Louis J. Vanrenen. *Bioenergetic Medicines East and West: Acupuncture and Homeopathy*. Berkeley, Calif.: North Atlantic Books, 1988.

Maslow, Abraham H. *Maslow on Management*. New York: John Wiley & Sons, 1998.

————. *Toward a Psychology of Being*, 3rd ed. New York: John Wiley & Sons, 1999.

Mauskopf, Seymour H., and Michael R. McVaugh. *The Elusive Science: Origins of Experimental Psychical Research*. Baltimore, Md.: Johns Hopkins University Press, 1980.

McMoneagle, Joseph. *Memoirs of a Psychic Spy: The Remarkable Life of U.S. Government Remote Viewer 001*. Charlottesville, Va.: Hampton Roads Publishing Co., 2006.

————. *Mind Trek: Exploring Consciousness, Time, and Space through Remote Viewing*. Charlottesville, Va.: Hampton Roads Publishing Co., 1997.

Mindell, Arnold. *Dreaming While Awake: Techniques for 24-Hour Lucid Dreaming*. Charlottesville, Va.: Hampton Roads Publishing Co., 2000.

Monroe, Robert. *Journeys Out of the Body*. New York: Doubleday, 1971.

Moody, Raymond. *Life After Life*. Harrisburg, Penn.: Stackpole Books, 1976.

Murphy, Michael, and Rhea A. White. *In the Zone: The Transcendent Experience in Sports*. New York: Penguin Books, 1995.

Myss, Caroline. *Anatomy of the Spirit: The Seven Stages of Power and Healing*. New York: Harmony Books, 1996.

Nahin, Paul J. *Time Travel*. Cincinnati, Ohio: Writer's Digest Books, 1997.

Oschman, James L. *Energy Medicine: The Scientific Basis*. Edinburgh, Scotland: Churchill Livingston, 2000.

Ouspensky, P. D. *The Fourth Way*. New York: Vintage Books, 1971.

Pearsall, Paul. *The Beethoven Factor: The New Positive Psychology of Hardiness, Happiness, Healing, and Hope*. Charlottesville, Va.: Hampton Roads Publishing Co., 2003.

Pert, Candace. *Molecules of Emotion*. New York: Scribner, 1997.

Petroski, Henry. *Design Paradigms: Case Histories of Error and Judgment in Engineering*. Cambridge, UK: Cambridge University Press, 1994.

Reber, Arthur S., and Emily Reber, eds. *The Penguin Dictionary of Psychology*, 3rd ed. London: Penguin Books, 1995.

Restak, Richard M. *The Brain: The Last Frontier*. New York: Warner Books, 1979.

Runes, Dagobert. *Dictionary of Philosophy*. Totowa, N.J.: Littlefield, Adams, and Co., 1980.

Sanchez, Victor. *The Toltec Path of Recapitulation: Healing Your Past to Free Your Soul*. Rochester, Vt.: Bear & Company, 2001.

Schopenhauer, Arthur. *The World as Will and Representation*, vols. 1, 2. Edited by E. F. J. Payne. New York: Dover Publications, 1969.

Sennett, Richard. *The Corrosion of Character: The Personal Consequences of Work in the New Capitalism*. New York: W. W. Norton & Co., 1998.

Sollars, David W. *The Complete Idiot's Guide to Acupuncture & Acupressure*. New York: Alpha Books, 2000.

Spencer, Sidney. *Mysticism in World Religion*. Gloucester, Mass.: Peter Smith, 1971.

Springer, Sally P., and Georg Deutsch. *Left Brain, Right Brain*, 4th ed. New York: W. H. Freeman and Co., 1993.

Stillings, Neil A., Steven E. Weisler, Christopher H. Chase, Mark H. Feinstein, Jay L. Garfield, and Edwina L. Rissland. *Cognitive Science*, 2nd ed. Cambridge, Mass.: MIT Press, 1995.

Suzuki, Shunryu. *Zen Mind, Beginner's Mind*. New York: Weatherhill, 1973.

Targ, Russell, and Jane Katra. *Miracles of Mind: Exploring Nonlocal Consciousness and Spiritual Healing*. Novato, Calif.: New World Library, 1998.

Tart, Charles T., ed. *Altered States of Consciousness*. New York: HarperCollins, 1990.

———. *Open Mind, Discriminating Mind: Reflections on Human Possibilities*. Lincoln, Neb.: www.iUniverse.com, Inc., 2000.

———. *States of Consciousness*. Lincoln, Neb.: www.iUniverse.com, Inc., 2000.

Trefil, James, ed. *Encyclopedia of Science and Technology*. New York: Routledge, 2001.

Whale, Jon. *The Catalyst of Power: The Assemblage Point of Man*. Findhorn, Scotland: Findhorn Press, 2001.

About the Author

Kenneth Smith, writing under the name Ken Eagle Feather, has published several books on Toltec philosophy, including *On the Toltec Path* and *Toltec Dreaming*. Concurrent with his apprenticeship to Toltec shaman don Juan Matus, he received degrees in education and mass communications/journalism from the University of Arizona and the University of South Florida, respectively. He later served on the staff of the Association for Research and Enlightenment, part of the Edgar Cayce legacy, and also on the staff of The Monroe Institute, founded by consciousness researcher Robert Monroe. He is the executive director for the Institute for Therapeutic Discovery, a medical science research organization, and lives in Richmond, Virginia.

Index

BOOKS OF RELATED INTEREST

On the Toltec Path
A Practical Guide to the Teachings of don Juan Matus, Carlos Castaneda,
and Other Toltec Seers
by Ken Eagle Feather

Toltec Dreaming
Don Juan's Teachings on the Energy Body
by Ken Eagle Feather

The Biology of Transcendence
A Blueprint of the Human Spirit
by Joseph Chilton Pearce

Radical Knowing
Understanding Consciousness through Relationship
by Christian de Quincey

The Chakras in Shamanic Practice
Eight Stages of Healing and Transformation
by Susan J. Wright

Shamanic Spirit
A Practical Guide to Personal Fulfillment
by Kenneth Meadows

Decoding the Human Body-Field
The New Science of Information as Medicine
by Peter H. Fraser and Harry Massey with Joan Parisi Wilcox

Vibrational Medicine
The #1 Handbook of Subtle-Energy Therapies
by Richard Gerber, M.D.

Inner Traditions • Bear & Company
P.O. Box 388
Rochester, VT 05767
1-800-246-8648
www.InnerTraditions.com

Or contact your local bookseller